LIFE
is
HARD
but
I'LL
BE
OK

The Power of **Hope**
Emerging *through Pain and*
Learning to Live with **Gratitude**

OVERCOMING GRIEF DURING THE CHALLENGES OF BUILDING A FAMILY

JOHNNY SIRPILLA

Life is Hard but I'll Be OK.
The Power of Hope Emerging through Pain and
Learning to Live with Gratitude

Johnny Sirpilla
Naples, FL 34110
Encourage33.com

In Association with:
Elite Online Publishing
63 East 11400 South #230
Sandy, UT 84070
EliteOnlinePublishing.com

ISBN: 978-1956642865 (eBook)
ISBN: 978-1956642872 (Paperback)

SEL010000
HEA045000

Praises for *Life is Hard but I'll be Ok*

"He has written a book to help anyone deal head-on with any struggle they face so they can become more resilient, eventually heal, and find beauty in the hardship, the silver lining in a dark cloud."

Dr. Nido Qubein, President of High Point University,
Author, Speaker, and award winner of
Horatio Alger Award for Distinguished Americans

"Johnny Sirpilla takes us on a journey through adversity and reminds us that anyone who is falling apart can put themselves together again at a higher level. With a heartwarming style of writing, he reminds us to find the blessings in our struggles and to explore our shadow selves so that we can live in a more whole and self-forgiving way. Touched by magic himself, Sirpilla will remind you that your own magic is more within your reach than you think. A profoundly touching page turner, this book is a must read."

Srini Pillay, M.D., Harvard-trained psychiatrist,
Chief Medical Officer and Co-Founder: Reulay

"This book embodies what life is about. If you're looking for a mindset shift or a life shift, this is the book that will give you that. Johnny shows us how to be resilient and how to see the beauty in anything that life throws at us. I'm glad to call him a friend and I thank him for these stories."

Bennie Fowler, Eight-year veteran of the NFL,
Super Bowl champion and Amazon bestselling author.

"To hold two emotions at once is one of the unique gifts of the human spirit. Johnny and Susan's powerful story gives us all hope that it is possible to experience joy amid pain and hope amid trial. *Life is Hard but I'll Be Ok* is poised to inspire you in whatever season of life you are currently in and prepare you for your next one!"

Dr. Amber Selking, Ph.D.,
VP Leadership & Culture of Lippert,
Author, & Founder of Selking Performance Group

"Too often, they met obstacles that dashed those dreams, or how they would have envisioned them. Their story is one of great joy, sorrow, perseverance, growth, and amazing faith."

Dr. Barb Fordyce, Ph.D., Public Speaker

"The application of the principles Johnny and Susan used to thrive rather than survive have life changing value to everyone. Whatever your struggle, this story is one of resilience and the power of managing thoughts to seek gratitude when life is hard. At a time when mental health is at the forefront of our society, this book is a must read."

Larry Dust, Founder and CEO of
American Health Data Institute

"Johnny and Susan have shared their incredibly personal and touching life experiences with a resounding clarity and honesty--yielding in us an opportunity, like it did for them, for a profound awakening"

Prab Gill, MD, FACOG, Maternal-Fetal Specialist

"Just as my good friend Johnny Sirpilla and his family learned through their personal tragedies and unthinkable losses, I leaned on God when everything in my life seemed to be difficult. The love of my family and my faith in Jesus Christ taught me that there are no bad days--only hard ones. Johnny and his family learned that *Life is Hard but I'll Be Ok.* Life isn't always going to be easy, but our faith in God--in good times and bad times--assures us that He is leading us to great things. Johnny's amazing story of perseverance is further proof of it."

JT Mestdagh, Author *No Bad Days*,
and *Untethered*, Public Speaker

"This fast paced, real-life story of an incredible journey toward parenthood inspires the reader with a heartwarming tale of faith, family, and perseverance."

Barbara and Jim Simmons
elected government official and former CEO and Chairman

DEDICATION

This book is dedicated to all those who struggle when life is hard and to those who provide strength and wisdom for the journey.

+

To my partner in our adventure for a family, my wife, Susan. You will soon understand the depths this woman endured to follow our hearts while fearlessly trusting in God along the way. This book is my tribute to her selfless spirit, unwavering determination, and fight to be a mother.

"Whatever our wound,

becomes our challenge.

Our task ... to walk

through the pain,

where we must look for the gift.

A gift that is there,

as reward for the trials."

Johnny Sirpilla

TABLE OF CONTENTS

FOREWORD

By Dr. Nido R. Qubein

Adversity can lead to abundance.

I tell that to our students, our parents, and our supporters in almost every speech I give at High Point University. When I see their quizzical looks, I mention that the hardships we face in life can temper us like a blacksmith tempers steel into a sword. Our hardships heighten our powers of observation, and it keeps us sharp, curious, and hungry in our drive for a better life for us and those around us.

I know Johnny Sirpilla has heard me say that before. He and his wife, Susan, are valued supporters of High Point University. I met them in 2014 when they joined the President's Leadership Council, and through their giving, they have created the Sirpilla Leadership Conference Room in HPU's Cottrell Hall. Even though they live hours away in Ohio and Florida, they always make a point to visit campus whenever they can. When they do, they're always a welcome sight to see.

Adversity is not something that comes to mind when I think of Johnny. He is always convivial, an immigrant's grandson, a second-generation Italian American who married his college sweetheart and went on to do well in business and in life. But Johnny knows about adversity firsthand, and his story will put your heart in your throat.

Just read his book you hold in your hands. *Life is Hard but I'll Be Ok* is quite the captivating read.

Johnny is a retired business executive, a leadership consultant, an active investor and entrepreneur, and a founding partner and advisor in legendary singer-songwriter Bob Dylan's spirit brand, Heaven's Door. Johnny is also a professional speaker who helps people reframe their life so they can tap into their passions and grow. Yet, he never saw himself as a writer. But as he shared his life story with friends and audiences everywhere, people would come up to him afterward always awed by what they heard.

"You have to write a book," they'd tell him. "Your story is almost too much to comprehend."

Now, he has. This is his first book.

Johnny writes about his life in such an incredibly honest way. He started his book in the fall of 2018, the year after retiring as former President and Chief Business Development Officer of Camping World, a nearly 200-store nationwide retail chain serving the RV industry. Johnny doesn't consider himself retired. He sees himself re-purposed on his life's ambitions. This time, though, he didn't have to help lead a company of 10,000 employees. He simply had to lead himself once again through the most traumatic events of his life that tested his faith. Some days, he wrote in a rush of words. Other days, though, he found that he needed weeks to process and prepare himself before jumping back into a story that made him quake.

His story reads like a novel. But that is Johnny's life.

Johnny told me Susan could always tell when he was back reliving those years and feeling so much all over again. He would be quiet, and Johnny is never quiet. Writing *Life is Hard but I'll Be OK* was hard. But it helped Johnny make sense of all that happened in his life he has shared with Susan. Throughout his book, he touches on themes of love and faith, resilience and resolve as he and Susan work tirelessly toward their lifelong dream.

They wanted to build a family together.

They experienced heartache and loss. But also joy. And self-discovery. And the importance to honor those now with God. Johnny and Susan honor one gut-wrenching loss with the release every year of three balloons — one pink; two blue. Then, right after a heartfelt prayer about needing a sign, Johnny felt three taps on his shoulder from a little baby boy he was cradling in his arms. Johnny knew that was a sign from God. He was listening.

From Johnny's compelling narrative about the journey he and Susan took, we all can see how we can heal from any traumatic event we face.

His book reminds me of what a curious teenager wrote decades ago as she hid with her family in a secret apartment in Amsterdam to escape detection from the Nazis. That teenager was Anne Frank, and her words in *The Diary of Anne Frank* show us all how writing can be the best medicine for the heart.

"I can shake off everything as I write," she once wrote. "My sorrows disappear, courage is reborn."

Johnny does know that now.

At High Point University, I use the phrase "faithful courage" in almost every speech I give. When I talk to the seniors the day before they graduate, I title my talk, "Onward with Faithful Courage." To understand 'faithful courage,' let's look at each word.

Faith is knowing what to do, trusting that sense of knowing and having faith in God.

As for the word "courage," that comes from the Latin root word for "heart." It has the same lineage as coronary. Your heart is your battery, your power source, and courage is your force of character to do it, no matter what the obstacle.

Taken together, these two qualities create a principled persistence that can help you overcome any adversary and beat any odds.

That is faithful courage. That is Johnny and Susan.

I have relied on faithful courage so many times in my own life. For example, at High Point University when COVID-19 kept us all on alert and anxious for months, I sent a quote to our faculty and staff to help ease their concern a few weeks before Christmas 2020. The quote came from Mother Angelica, the entrepreneurial Catholic nun from Canton,

Ohio, who used $200 to create the world's largest religious media network at a monastery in Birmingham, Alabama. She said: "Faith is what gets you started. Hope is what keeps you going. Love is what brings you to the end."

I do believe that with all my heart. All things are possible for those who have faith.

So, whenever I face a hardship that could drop me to my knees, I don't ever lose hope. I know the faithful company of those I love and trust will support me. I also think of the verse from 1 Corinthians: "So that your faith might not rest in the wisdom of men, but in the power of God."

Johnny and Susan know that, too.

So, enjoy *Life is Hard but I'll Be Ok.* Ironically, Johnny got the title from speaking years ago to a business class at High Point University. The title came from his answer to a question a student asked him. And look what happened. He has written a book to help anyone deal head-on with any struggle they face so they can become more resilient, eventually heal, and find beauty in the hardship, the silver lining in a dark cloud.

So, I implore you to look for what lessons you'll take away from Johnny's book. You will. You'll also find passages that will stick with you long after you've closed "Life is Hard ... But I'll Be Okay." Here is one:

"This wasn't just our moment, it belonged to our village that carried us on the days that we couldn't think of walking, loved us when our thoughts were so dark that we couldn't feel love, and encouraged us to be faithful to our focus to build a family without consideration for leaving each other or our dreams. I don't know if I have ever delivered news that brought people to a level of relief, bliss, and love as I did in this experience. It was magical."

What was that news? Read on. You'll find out. And you, too, will see it as magical.

Dr. Nido R. Qubein is the president of High Point University. He became the university's president in 2005. Since then, he has spearheaded a $3 billion investment in the university that has helped open eight new academic schools, quadruple the number of faculty as well as the size of the campus and the student body. That work has helped the university become the South's No. 1 regional college for the past decade, according to U.S. News & World Report. Dr. Qubein has written a dozen books, ran six companies, started a bank, and consulted CEOs. He serves on the national boards of Truist Financial, nThrive, and Great Harvest Bread Co. He is also a philanthropist, entrepreneur and a highly sought-after speaker who has received many awards, including the Horatio Alger Award for Distinguished Americans, along with the late Colin Powell and Oprah Winfrey.

The Question

In so many ways it was typical. Yet in another way it was extraordinary.

I was invited to speak to the business students at High Point University in High Point, North Carolina. The Business School had combined the classes together—accounting, marketing, management, finance, etc., assembling into one large gathering in one of their pristine lecture halls.

The HPU campus is beautiful—one of the most beautiful in the country. Speaking at many college campuses, I take particular note of the setting and personality that can be felt surrounded by the young minds of our future. There was a natural fit and comfort that day, as this university proudly displays their values of God, family, and country. I'm aligned, comfortable and inspired.

HPU is known as a Premiere Life Skills University and my talk would tie back to the school's mission; developing life skills in our journey that defined the business life I would lead. The university welcomes the union of faith, business, and person. I felt right at home.

It was the autumn of 2019, September 19th to be exact. It was a bit early for the colored leaves to be in peak form, but the reds, golds and yellows were just beginning to present themselves in the beauty of a North Carolina fall. If one breathed in deeply, you could catch the faint smell of the pine needles that were used in the landscaping on the campus, giving it that feel of southern charm on the grounds. The sun was shining, the sky was clear, it was a warm day, but since I was inside, the air conditioning made it close to perfect.

At precisely 11:40 am I was introduced by the Dean of the business school, Dr. Jim Wehrley. Excitedly, I stood at the front of the room to address the students, who numbered into the hundreds. The room was a large amphitheater— levels of seats moving higher and higher from the front of the room to the rear. The walls were crisp white, with the only addition being a large screen behind me at the front.

Speaking to large crowds was not an uncommon assignment for me. I had been doing it for years, making it one of the centerpieces of my company, Encourage LLC. It is even highlighted on the bio page of my website:

Johnny speaks professionally to businesses, communities, and universities on the importance of managing thoughts, internal honest reflection to develop meaningful professional and personal relationships, and re-framing each challenge in your life as an opportunity for self-development and growth. Addressing college students and young professionals to discover the power they must develop in their personal brand is a passion and target audience for Johnny.

So, there was really no reason to suspect that this speaking engagement was going to be any different than the many I had done before it.

As was my normal routine, I assured the group that I welcome interruptions when I speak. I'm a firm believer in "seek to understand" when engaging with others which to me means that sometimes we must push ourselves to understand because it may not digest naturally. So, I invite the audience to challenge me in their quest to seek to understand the messages that I'm giving and if something doesn't hit their ear right, I want to seek to understand why. It gives me a chance to reframe the message, clarify if I wasn't clear or provide confirmation to them that they are not in agreement with me, which is okay.

In this venue the students politely raised their hands, were acknowledged, and asked their questions of me. Again, very typical. I had been through this program countless times before.

But it was when a young man asked me the following question that the situation moved to an exceptional moment.

"What do you wish you knew when you were sitting in my seat that would have prepared you for the life that you were going to lead?"

As I stood in front of that collegiate crowd, I looked out to the hundreds of hopeful eyes looking back up to me, awaiting my answer to this seemingly simple query.

During discussions like this, I am comfortable with and encourage open dialogue, hopeful that students ask questions just as this young man did. However, at this moment, the wisdom and intensity of his question struck me differently than the previous inquiries. As I sifted through my head for an adequate answer, I consciously recognized that this moment would act as an anchor I would return to in making many life-altering decisions in the future.

My response came out of my mouth before it reached my mind. That can often lead to trouble, but in this case, I found a sense of purpose in all that our family had been through in our lives that I hadn't even realized had been missing. This genesis prompted me to begin writing the book you hold in your hands.

I think back to that answer often, wondering if what I imparted to them might've been too deflating, too distilled for the room of intelligent and impressionable college students sitting in front of me. As a speaker, I had just spent the last hour explaining the ins and outs of life as if I held inside of me a handbook that would guide them to success. I listed the exact tools needed to create their own success and the truly simple ways to avoid the pitfalls in crafting a meaningful life, backing these up with handpicked experiences and anecdotes. I never intended for the audience to draw that based on my own individual challenges, the information I imparted should serve as any more than mere suggestions from a guest lecturer, let alone an individualized and prescriptive outline of the hacks to a good life. In fact, despite what appears to be a charmed life by onlookers, I, along with many others, sit in a world of blessings with so much pain and emotion below the surface. What I didn't mention in my lecture were the many times I was required to dig deeply to find the blessings in my struggles and find peace with my demons so my family could flourish.

+ + +

Frankly, I don't remember exactly how long it took me to open my mouth to give this young man an answer to his question. In some ways, it felt like I answered him almost immediately. But in other ways, I remember it as time standing still—a seeming eternity between being asked and offering an answer.

"What do you wish you knew when you were sitting in my seat that would have prepared you for the life that you were going to lead?"

As I have often said, there is no conversation that is too uncomfortable given that it is approached with honesty, integrity, and genuine respect for others. Holding this core value so closely to me, I decided it would not be fair to avoid the truth. Rather, however blunt and distilled it may have seemed, I chose to acknowledge my responsibility to share the wisdom I have derived from my times of trial. I chose to repeat a mantra I have lived by, held on to, and anchored myself to in my worst lows:

"Life is hard, but I'll be OK."

In this simple answer, I hoped to embody the following message: Your dreams for the future may become clouded. No matter how frightening they might seem, your toughest times never lie in the rearview mirror but instead, are waiting at the next stop ahead.

This book is an outpouring of the emotions and thoughts behind our story. In no way are my words meant to elicit any sympathy or exude the thought that we have had it worse than others. In fact, as I write, I am painfully aware that my wife and I both grew up with so many blessings. Regardless, I write about these unbearably painful experiences in hopes that I can share the ways reflection, the reconfiguration of thoughts, and mental stamina can keep us moving forward.

Given the fact that much of my story regards experiences with my wife, Susan, I will be referring to us as a unit, and at other times, I will be reflecting solely from my perspective. While I choose to make this differentiation at times, I truly don't have clarity to know whether my feelings are a result of her feelings or my own. Maybe this is one of the benefits of having a soul mate with you on your journey through life.

It is said that it takes a village to raise a child, and in my opinion, that village holds the responsibility of support and shaping the individual throughout his or her entire life. I know that I could not have come through my darkness without drawing from the faith and strength from those I have met in my many villages. As matter of fact, as I think about the man I am today, I realize that I am unable to view myself as a single being all my own. My core is made up of every person I have ever respected, loved, or learned from. I am who I am because I have witnessed those I love and respect most as they stand up when it was most natural to fall down. With this in mind, I ask you to come along this journey with me as I talk about the joy, pain, tragedy and life lessons that have allowed me to find peace.

Standing in the front of that lecture hall on that sunny North Carolina September afternoon turned out to be an exceptional moment in my life. That curious student led me to articulate an eight-word declaration that encapsulates the many years I had already lived. With my answer, I hoped to offer something profound, yet tangible, practical, and worthy of application.

We are all here to discover our purpose, live our best lives, and accept the answer to our most fateful moments … *"Life is hard, but I'll be OK."*

What follows is how that phrase played itself out in our lives. Here's our story…

CHAPTER 1

Can This Much Happiness Be Real?

There's nothing happier than a wedding.

Susan and I were married on June 1, 1991. There was plenty going on in the world that year. The Gulf War ended, Bush and Gorbachev were hashing out a strategic arms reduction treaty, the Giants beat the Bills in Super Bowl XXV, with Whitney Houston singing the National Anthem and New Kids on the Block performing at halftime. Most Americans were watching *Cheers*, *Murphy Brown* and *Seinfeld* on TV, viewing *Dances With Wolves* and *Beauty and the Beast* at the movie theater, and listening to the music of Mariah Carey, Phil Collins and Bryan Adams.

All that information is really just a blur to me, for the center of my universe was our wedding venue, St. Bernard's Cathedral in downtown Akron, Ohio. We were later told it was the largest wedding held at that church, with close to 500 people in attendance. Imagine 25 of those 500 people standing at the altar—our Priest, the Bride and Groom, and 11 bridesmaids and 11 groomsmen!

Add to that mental picture some serious heat—temperatures in the 90's in a structure without air conditioning.

There's more to our wedding that I want you to know, but first, let's introduce you to the main characters in our Love Story.

+ + +

If you drive for miles and miles through the farmlands of the state of Ohio, eventually you will happen upon the campus of Miami University or also known as Miami of Ohio. It's located in Oxford -- a classic college town lined with red brick streets "uptown", consistent red brick architecture, and famous for the beauty of its campus.

I met my wife, Susan, in the final weeks of our senior year at that university. Our first date was more like a weekend, full of various activities and venues, seeing one another in a variety of environments.

There was a fraternity/sorority party set for that weekend---the centerpiece for our meeting. As president of my fraternity, I was confident that we were going to create lasting memories as our college experience was coming to a close.

The night before the date party, the seniors of Alpha Chi Omega (AXΩ) and Sigma Alpha Epsilon (SAE) met together for a "fire up" before our shared party. The venue was a local bar called *Bangs*. And that is where I met Susan. (I smile when I think back on that meeting, because our prim and proper mothers blushed with embarrassment when we're asked where we met and we smile broadly and reply, "We met at bar called *Bangs!*")

Susan recalls how formal I was in introducing myself. "Hello, I'm John Sirpilla," I said, as I held out my hand to shake hers. Susan had seen me before—at church my freshman year, but it took all those years in between for us to finally connect for real.

We spent a lot of time together that weekend. At the party, I was dancing with another girl that Susan was friends with and Susan joined in … the other girl eventually moved on. We ended up talking at the windowsill of my fraternity house until 3am.

A quick note for perspective. That windowsill conversation provided the first look into the woman that Susan would become and what led her so naturally to accept all that would happen to her. Her mother was widowed at the age of 25 with three young children. She put herself through school while charting a course to recreate her life after tragedy; even went on to get her masters. Years later, she remarried, had Susan, and lived a life of strength with grace. I have admired that in others and I'm reminded of my sweet mother-in-law who I miss dearly today. The night I met Susan, I was attracted to the grace and strength she acquired from her mother. I see it so clearly now how she had my heart that night in the way she exuded an energetic, calming power that I would come to rely on for my own survival.

Back to the fraternity setting. I was taking a friend to the date party the next night, but I had a connection with Susan so Saturday morning, I found my dear friend another date and I asked Susan. I even picked her up for mass that Sunday.

Susan would later confess, "At first, I thought Johnny was a little too much *Italian Stallion* for me, (I confess, I did have a framed picture of Rocky hung prominently in my room) but I began to see much more than that."

I wasn't a fighter or a troublemaker, but if I saw injustice at play, I would jump in to defend the victims. At the date party, I saw a guy come on to our front lawn and disrespect a fraternity brother's girlfriend, so I proceeded to find the guy in the front yard of the fraternity house and — let's just say I more than encouraged him to leave with strong authority. That probably added to Susan's vision of me as a *Guido* from a *Godfather* movie.

Our relationship formed effortlessly, both of us bonding over a childhood steeped in the Catholic faith, a shared love of our times on the tennis court, and a passion for the future.

We both enjoyed very comfortable childhoods, feeling loved, supported, and even prioritized by our committed parents. We grew up thirty minutes apart in northeastern Ohio, but it took being five hours from home at Miami University to find each other. We realized the blessings in our parents' strictness, the guardrails they insisted we stay within, and their constant support. We were part of the lucky ones who felt loved, supported, and encouraged throughout our entire lives. Both of us feel eternally grateful and attribute the many successes in both our work and family lives to these solid foundations.

I grew up in a classic Italian family. I was the youngest child, with two older sisters ahead of me. My sisters, Renae and Laura are only 13 months apart, but Dad really wanted a son. When each of my sisters were born, he would announce, "Little Johnny is wearing a skirt!" which was his way of saying he had a daughter. My dad adored my sisters and was a typical Italian father of two girls—very protective.

Dad had six years of convincing to get my mom to have another baby, and eventually I was born on October 7, 1966. I weighed a hefty 10 pounds, 7 ounces at birth, making it easy to remember—born on 10/7, weighing 10/7. It was not an easy delivery for my mom and in truth, the entire pregnancy was a challenge. Instead of gaining weight, as most pregnant women do, my mom *lost* five pounds while she was pregnant with me.

My dad pioneered the Recreational Vehicle industry and was one of the first RV dealers in the country in the late 1950's. As a young man, he and his brother, bought a gas station right out of high school in 1950 and started renting tent campers in 1959. Dad never attended college, although he did take one college class -- Dale Carnegie's *How to Win Friends and Influence People*. He did that masterfully.

My mom stayed at home with us while being an extraordinary community leader, starting the local Catholic college's women's league and the Catholic hospital's women's service league. In her late 40's she started a clothing store with my sister, Laura, and started working full time. Today, she is 84 years old and she still works 6 days a week at Laura of Pembroke; a cornerstone business in our community styling women and offering full service home interior design, accessories and furnishings.

I approached college with the same intensity I carried throughout the beginning portion of my life. I worked hard, envisioning myself juggling countless job offers by the fall of my senior year so I could land the job of my dreams in the city of my choice. I worked hard to build an impressive resume, achieve remarkable grades, and gain the work experience that would set me up for a prosperous future.

When I met Susan five weeks before graduation, I discovered that there was another way to approach life and still achieve greatness. She lived in the moment and still acted responsibly. She seemed to trust in the way life unfolded itself, following a casual approach to the job search life after school. Upon seeing the mellow approach to the future, I felt mildly alarmed. My first instinct was to help her "catch up" to the place I felt I was at, strategizing and outlining plans for her future. As opposed to being alarmed, I should have seen our unique styles to handling the future as the first sign of the equilibrium that would sustain us in what was ahead. Within a month of graduation, she landed a very competitive job in the pharmaceutical industry, earning a salary significantly higher than mine, along with better benefits and a company car. Her future was bright, and she earned success without asking for my outlines or strategic guidance.

We returned to Akron and Canton, Ohio after graduation and spent the next few months enjoying our time together before our careers would inevitably separate us. I was moving to Chicago, and she was willing to take any pharmaceutical territory in the country to pioneer her future. She was disappointed to learn that she was assigned to her hometown in Akron, thus not getting the opportunity to move away and experience living in a different part of the country. In an era, sans cell phones, we chose to avoid the challenges of a long-distance relationship and embrace our futures as independent young adults.

Before I embarked on my journey to Chicago, we shared a tearful goodbye, even though we had only dated four months. We found comfort in the fact that if it were a part of God's plan, our paths might cross again in the future. We separated, knowing that no matter how hard this goodbye was, starting a new life deserved our full attention. I can remember that night as if it were yesterday and can still feel the anxiety as I left her, my mind racing about whether we had done the right thing.

Over a year later, I was enjoying the early signs of success in Chicago when I received a phone call from my father. He requested that I return home to join the family RV business. My dad pioneered a business in the RV industry and touted a gold-plated reputation as one of the top dealers in Ohio and the Midwest. I respected him as a businessman and as a father, so when he encouraged me to pursue an undergraduate degree in accounting, I obliged. I never held any intention of becoming an accountant, but I trusted my dad in guiding me towards an area of study that could contribute to future success. Gaining experience from founding and operating a business, my dad understood how accounting, and more broadly a solid education, served as the underlying currency of business. As a first-generation Italian hailing from immigrant parents, he was not afforded the luxury of higher education and learned the world of business on the fly, all while sustaining a decent sized company. Even though I was living the exciting post-graduate life that I had sought after for so long, I remember the simplicity of the conversation. My reply came easily, "OK, Pops." The thought of disappointing my parents and failing to live up to their expectations was a chance I was not willing to take. In October of 1989, I moved home to Canton and my life quickly progressed from there.

My first call was to Susan with hopes that she was still single and interested in spending time together. Thankfully, she was, and our relationship picked up right where we had tearfully left it just 16 months before. Within a few months, I was buying an engagement ring. Over the years, I have asked my parents why they would allow me to propose so quickly at 23 years old to someone I dated for such a short time. My mom's reply has remained consistent for thirty years, "There was nothing to stop. She was the one for you." Having the support of my parents and two older sisters was everything to me. The way that they loved and embraced Susan made me love her even more.

+ + +

Wedding preparations for a party of over 500 people wasn't stressful, but rather, the process reaffirmed our love for one another and prepared our two loving families to join. On June 1, 1991, we became one and the love story of our married life began. We wrote our own wedding vows with intention, forming a contract at the altar. In retrospect, our most impactful vow was, "I promise to see your viewpoint in all, as you must see mine." Writing and reading those words aloud to one another at 24 years old served as a foundation that would sustain us in the challenges ahead. I'm so thankful that we made our pledges to one another in the presence of God. Life was soon going to hand us many situations that would require us to look to one another with mutual respect and understanding. The value we placed in considering each other's views served as a cornerstone to our marriage, supporting us in remaining united even in times of trial.

Most married couples have a story or two to tell about something out of the ordinary that occurred during the wedding or reception. Our wedding party got off to a bumpy beginning.

Most wedding parties are driven to the church in a caravan of limousines or town cars. Not us. Since my dad was so proud of his RV business, we were driven to the church in brand new RVs, top of the line, state of the art. This RV caravan included both sets of parents and the large wedding party. Susan's mom was excitedly standing in the stairwell of the RV which is not well advised. While driving down the interstate, the entry door flew open, and my future mother-in-law nearly fell out of the RV moving 65+ mph. Quick action from the strong women safely held on to her while shutting the door in a fast-moving vehicle. My mother-in-law was un-phased which demonstrated the rock that she was in our lives.

We had another "unusual circumstance" that occurred during the actual wedding ceremony.

In the Catholic ceremony, there is a point when the bride walks to the statue of the Blessed Mother while the *Ave Maria* plays. The bride offers a bouquet of flowers to Mary, symbolizing the bride offering herself to Mary to obtain her intercession for a fruitful spousal love. It is a significant gesture which honors Mary as Virgin and Mother and expresses binding with her for a new stage of life.

I escorted Susan to the left side of the altar, to the base of the Blessed Mother statue as that most beautiful song was playing. As Susan knelt before Mary, I stepped back, and began my own prayers for us to be blessed with children.

Since it was so blistering hot in the church, the front doors had remained open in hopes of circulating some cooler air (it didn't help). At the exact time we were both praying, a police car sped past the church, sirens blaring, and the sound echoed throughout the sanctuary, drowning out the music and thoroughly disrupting this intense moment of prayer for children.

I just tilted my head back and smiled. After the ceremony we laughed and joked about it, saying the sirens were a warning sign for our family planning. As you'll read, it turned out to not be so funny.

We had so many people warning us of trials that we might face in the first year of marriage and as a result, Susan and I grew increasingly confused. We found happiness every day, finding excitement in returning home after work to be with one another with our respective to do lists for a successful marriage and life together. Many times, we turned to each other and asked, "Are we really supposed to be this happy?" "How can we be worthy of such good fortune in our careers, our supportive families and friendships that we knew would last a lifetime?"

We formed friendships with couples who shared in our faith and ideals, unaware that these people would become family and serve as our support system in the years to come. Our careers were on a fast track to success, and I continued to take pride that Susan was earning more money than me, never shying to brag about her success. We saved every penny that she earned and lived off my income, remaining disciplined to keep debt low and savings high. We felt blessed, and we made time to thank God for this incredible start to our lives together.

This part of our life story is important to tell, to set a foundation and provide insight to the solid upbringings, friendships, faith, and finances that played an integral role in the turbulent times that laid ahead. We attended mass faithfully, and we felt blessed to be able to handle whatever life may throw at us. As prepared as we felt in these earlier years, the times ahead would require us to rely heavily on the strengths of our support system. With the help of our friend, psychologist and partner Dr. Barbara Fordyce, Susan and I realized the value in thought management techniques and the ways in which these can drive our future choices in the right direction. It is my hope that in relaying our story, we can share the importance of these techniques, so that you may benefit from her methodology.

Life was good. Yet, in our case, as happy as we were in those early days, there was a secret we were carrying that was threatening our joy.

John B. (Dad), Laura (sister), Johnny,
Renae (sister), Veronica (Mom)

First date

CHAPTER 2

A Secret Develops

On the outside, things seemed perfect for Susan and me. But we had a secret.

And it was a secret that came with a flood of negative emotions.

Fear.

Is this going to be my life?

Disappointment.

This is not what my spouse wants, and I feel responsible.

Guilt.

Knowing how much we wanted this aspect of our marriage to blossom, we didn't blame each other, rather we blamed ourselves.

Our secret?

We wanted to have children and for some unexplained reason, it wasn't coming to pass.

+ + +

As our careers continued to thrive and we enjoyed building our first home, we began to feel ready to take that next step in our relationship. A year into our marriage, at the age of 25, we felt it was time to start our family. I knew that getting Susan to join me in my dream of having six children was going to be a challenge, but I remained hopeful. (I'll have more to say about this subject later.)

Our family and friends had no idea that our hearts were anywhere near the place of becoming parents. The strong focus that we held on to our careers seemed to indicate that we would not want any distraction from achieving our financial and career goals. We felt content with how we were perceived and discretely began our journey to parenthood.

As a goal-oriented and extremely motivated couple, the idea of creating a baby with God's grace seemed to be well within our grasps. We educated ourselves on exactly what to do, what days of the month to do it, and when to expect the good news. It was a happy time as we talked with certainty of our future children.

After our first month of concerted effort, we stood together eager to celebrate a positive pregnancy test.

Negative.

We stood shocked. We were surprised, and we felt the initial seeds of insecurity implanted in our minds. However, it was far too early in the journey to legitimize these feelings, and it was easy to privately dismiss without discussing it. We knew it would be ridiculous to complain or even feel disappointed. After all the blessings that we had enjoyed throughout our lives, we were more than fine. Or so I told myself.

No matter how many times I repeated these reassurances, thoughts began to race through my head about the reasons as to why, despite doing everything right (and often) and remaining faithful to God, we did not receive the results we expected. Unsure of what laid ahead, I felt a harsh sense of failure after the first month. I remained stuck in the mentality I carried throughout school, athletics and in business. Set a goal, take the proper steps, achieve the goal, set the next goal and repeat. My perceived failure took me back to the drawing board. I reassured myself by thinking, "There are less enjoyable tasks to have to repeat, right?"

Several months followed, each one greeting us with another negative test. Inevitably, within a few days of taking the test, "Aunt Flo" would arrive. We named and began to creatively refer to Susan's menstrual cycle as Aunt Flo, speaking of her as if she were an unwanted house guest that kept paying us a visit each month. Every family just must have that one relative that drives them crazy, right? Aunt Flo was that relative to us and warding her off became a commonplace in our conversation.

Things became more complicated as our friends began announcing their pregnancies. We shared in their excitement and held onto our secret that we had been trying. We felt genuinely happy with their immediate success resulting in a healthy pregnancy and genuinely celebrated with them. As couples, we were all in the same position; deeply in love, working hard, and enjoying many blessings. In public, we expressed the only emotion acceptable … joy.

However, in private, Susan and I started to open up about thoughts that raced through our minds that we felt were unacceptable to share with others. As more and more pregnancy announcements came, Susan confided in me that she had always heard a voice in the back of her mind that told her that she would have a difficult time getting pregnant. She said she didn't want to scare me with the thought or surround our attempts with negative energy, but she was becoming scared that she had always known that this was her fate.

Following her honest confession, I revealed to her that I always knew that I would be a dad but just couldn't see myself as a biological dad. Often in high school and college I tried to envision myself with children, but I just could never envision a biological connection in terms of believing that I would have biological children. There was always a block in my mind that I could never seem to get around. In a more honest place, we continued our attempts. We rationalized our fears away and tried to suppress a self-fulfilling prophecy that was appearing to become our reality.

Through research, we learned that some couples need a little more assistance in becoming pregnant. Armed with new information on some techniques that might increase the likelihood of a pregnancy, we dutifully charted Susan's daily temperature and meticulously arranged pillows (attempting to be a gentleman and not get into details). We altered our methods, realizing that pregnancy is a life altering event and that anything worth having was worth the wait. Charts and thermometers became permanent fixtures on our nightstand table. Some months teased us, and we were often fooled by Susan's period delaying several days or arriving hours after the test. We closed out the first year of our pregnancy endeavor with twelve negative tests in hand. Twelve months with the same conversation between us.

"Negative," Susan would announce.

"Next month will be different," I replied.

"Yes, it's going to happen," Susan would agree, yet added, "But I want it to happen *now*."

We pushed any notion of discouragement aside and readied ourselves for year two.

+ + +

As the universe would have it, when you desperately want something, you are drawn to notice your dream being actualized through the lives of others. Seeing pregnant teenagers while on trips to the shopping mall provoked downwardly spiral-like thoughts of why unplanned pregnancies seemed so easy to achieve.

Regardless, we refused to embrace the thought of *"Why us?"* and centered our dialogue around *"Why not us?"*

We were so blessed, so we viewed our failed attempts at pregnancy as a light cross to bear in the grand scheme of things. We loved each other, we remained committed to each other, and we refused to waiver.

Innocent and well-intentioned questions became more frequent as we approached our third year of marriage, and any talk of children remained off the table for both of us. We continued to show genuine happiness for our friends as they welcomed their first child, and we felt so honored to be selected as godparents for two families. Our well-kept secret made it easier to be genuine in our happiness for other couples. They did not select us as godparents as a gesture of empathy, rather because of our love for them, the Lord, and their baby. That is exactly how we wanted it.

During friends' pregnancies, we tried our best to fight off thoughts surrounding when our day might come. We realized that their announcements should center around their happiness, and the joy of those moments belonged to the expecting couple. Each couple celebrating their exciting news had loved and supported us in so many ways, so it was truly a happy time watching families around us grow. We saw the potential in what we might someday receive painted so clearly in countless friends' lives. Our love for them truly sustained us during that time because we were thrilled for their happiness. In many ways, they lifted us up without knowing it because they gave us joy.

Year two required a new game plan, and I felt that it was my responsibility to spearhead this change. Susan needed to relax and allow her body to be prepared for pregnancy. I didn't want her to feel an ounce of stress about setting up doctor appointments, doing research, or wondering if we might have a medical problem. It was stressful enough to live with me as an active thinker (later to be diagnosed with anxiety) and a guy who likes to express his feelings and talk … a lot.

I scheduled an appointment at her OBGYN office to clear her head of worries. Despite our overall wellbeing and good health, intense emotions and fear followed us into our first visit. While we sought to understand the source of our challenge, we dreaded the fact that we could be walking into fateful and life altering news. Nevertheless, we continued. We both underwent some initial testing, and all results returned completely normal. At this, we were told that our problem with our infertility was unexplained, and we may need just a little medical intervention to assist with conception. Since it had been over a year of attempts, medical protocol suggested that we take next steps—artificial insemination and if that didn't work, invitro fertilization which was highly unlikely for us due to the good news on the medical testing.

As practicing Catholics, we knew the church's stance on procedural impregnation, and we felt the weight of their verdict heavily in our decision. Simply, the church believes that removing God from the marital act of creation and involving medical procedures violates the intended way of conception. We prayed about whether to accept medical help because this was a true dilemma for us. We spoke with our priest who did not take a hard stance against medical intervention, which eased our concerns. In the end, we felt that God knew our hearts, and we chose to move forward with the doctor's recommendations. We were truly naïve as to the challenges that awaited us which were unimaginable and far reaching into levels of depth that were life threatening. I will address those issues in later chapters.

As with any unfortunate time in our lives, there is good fortune all around us if we are willing to realize it. In the midst of our struggles, I began my first year of a national leadership program. Leadership Canton was a fairly new program that enrolled committed members of the community in a two-year seminar series to equip them with knowledge to better serve the community. One day per month for a full year, we spent a day dedicated to learning about the various critical components of our community. Leadership Canton acted as a bright patch in this era of my life and offered an incredible way to reflect on my role in cultural diversity, education, health care, social service, our judicial system, mental health, and other critical topics impacting our community. It was through these seminars that I developed a keen interest in mental health and the ways in which our attitudes can affect outcomes. On one day in particular, the key-note speaker featured Dr. Barbara Fordyce, who owned the largest and most respected psychology practice in town. The words that she spoke in her presentation that day laid the foundation for a method of critical thinking that I have relied heavily on for over two decades. We quickly formed a friendship, and I realized that Dr. Fordyce's message was critical in my journey of creating lifelong mental health. This introduction to thought management and reframing thoughts spurred my interest in returning to school to earn my master's degree in organizational behavioral management.

I came home from the mental health leadership seminar exploding with excitement. I was eager to share with Susan that to get through the next phase of our infertility, we needed professional help from Dr. Fordyce. Susan's loving spirit quickly agreed and over the many sessions ahead, Dr. Fordyce, became Barb to us as she laid the principles that would keep us resilient for the journey ahead. We learned to hold a clear focus on maintaining the strength of our relationship independently of whether we conceived. We were conscious of the hard reality that many infertile couples choose to end their marriage prior to conception. We set a clear goal to avoid becoming a part of this statistic and chose to approach our troubles as one unit rather than individuals. Barb helped us understand that while we each may express our emotions differently, anything other than love and supporting messages to each other was unacceptable. Following the same game plan that had facilitated our previous achievements, we formed goals and an emotional plan to face the wave of feelings that might result from any unintentionally offensive comments that might come our way. Barb, our new partner for the journey ahead, facilitated a safe space for open dialogue about any thoughts that created anxiety and emotion. I often joked with Barb that if she only knew what was ahead of her in the next twenty plus years, she may have wished she wasn't so powerful in her Leadership Canton presentation. She was too gracious to deny the friendship that we had formed and took pride in knowing that she was a critical element in letting us be heard, rooted in love and ready for the cross that we were carrying.

Feeling emotionally stable and supported by her, we entered the artificial insemination process hopeful and accepting of the fact that creating our baby had transpired into more of a medical procedure than an expressed act of love. We faced that reality head on, and we didn't need to attach emotion around this required adjustment. It was what it was, and we were thankful for assistance to fulfill the dream of parenthood.

Finally, the day we had prepared for and spoke so long about arrived. As we were separated into different rooms for the mutual preparation of the procedure, we accepted our choice and prayed. We tried to think our positive hopes into existence. Everything was aligned--we knew with certainty we did not have medical concerns that required correction, all ultrasounds confirmed that the egg follicle was in fact there and ready for conception, and our minds were in a better place than ever. We eagerly awaited day 14 of Susan's cycle as the magical day for insemination so our baby could be created and then patiently waited for two weeks for the big news. Knowing that we didn't have a specific medical issue, the assurance of a healthy egg joined with sperm at the right time would logically lead to pregnancy. We couldn't wait for the two weeks to pass and take the test.

However, on day 28, testing day, we were greeted with yet another negative pregnancy test.

Tears flowed and our deeply rooted anxieties grew, but we returned the next month. And the next month. And the next. Each time we faced a negative pregnancy test, we recalled the enormity of what we were attempting to do--create a human life. This should not be a simple process.

Our secret became more difficult to conceal as we spent so much time together in the OBGYN's office. We remained so dedicated to our pact of secrecy that after befriending the receptionists, we gained access to the back entrance in hopes of avoiding anyone we might know in the lobby.

After months of failed inseminations, our doctor felt it was time to add a drug called Pergonal into the equation. Although Susan was producing follicles presumably with eggs, the drug would increase Susan's egg production and increase the likelihood of pregnancy. We didn't question it. What's another step in the process? We didn't draw a line where our commitment ended, so it was just the next step. Something in my being told me that this was wrong, but again, we accepted that our journey did not have to be easy, and we chose to stay the course. Anything worth having is worth fighting for, right? As an infertile couple, which was how we were now defined, our lives revolved around the days of Susan's cycles and the time of day in which I needed to give her shots for egg production.

That first shot remains as clear in my mind as it was more than 28 years ago. We were heading to a summer concert with friends and were at a party prior to the concert. We were told countless times that staying on schedule was critical to successful conception, and it just so happened that the time of our first injection was during the party. We quietly slipped away into the bathroom of our friend's home. I diligently recited the instructions of how to withdraw the drug from the vial, ensuring no bubbles remained in the syringe. Willing to put her body through whatever was needed, Susan handled the pain like a champ and accepted this new first step better than I did, (you will notice a trend of this happening in our lives).

I tried to steady myself as my nerves were getting to me and everything inside of me told me that injecting these drugs into her body was not the ultimate answer for us. Sure, it was getting us a step closer to becoming parents but at what cost? As an "active thinker", which is the term I would soon use for my anxiety diagnosis of the future, my mind raced to the impact that fertility drugs could have on breast cancer or other cancers. I've always been one to think of five chess moves out, so I can guarantee a win. Seeing what is right in front of me seems so short sighted, because I recognize that there are countless consequences to our choices. I am always painfully aware that my first move must be in respect to the following moves, so I am never caught off guard with an undesirable outcome. Combine that "active thinking" with some control freak tendencies, and well, you can imagine the joy that I was to Susan during this process. In fairness to myself, my concerns typically were rooted in a reality that we experienced. Eighteen years later Susan needed a double mastectomy at the age of 44. While a story for another day, the thought deep within me may have had some truth to it.

Back to the first shot. It took several attempts to actually inject the shot into her skin, because each time, I would pull back in fear before the needle touched her skin. Eventually, I successfully got the needle in and administered the Pergonal.

Instead of feeling a sense of accomplishment, my emotion hit me like a train, and tears soon followed.

Tears of admiration, alarm, and anxiety.

Tears of admiration that my wife was willing to compliantly follow along with this painful process in hopes of one day being a mother. Tears of alarm for the potential harm the drug might cause twenty years in the future. And simply tears of anxiety for potentially another negative pregnancy test in four weeks.

We had introduced the next step in the process. As a couple with no medical reason for infertility, we were just the ones that needed a little help. We pushed our fears aside for the hope that in one month of the egg producing drug for Susan (and tear producing drug for me) we would have our long-awaited pregnancy. We couldn't wait for the results so that maybe our secret life could end, and the blessing of becoming parents would be ours. With smiles on our faces and tears in our eyes, we knew it was all worth it and were just ready for that next pregnancy test.

Negative ... again.

Crushed but not totally defeated, we repeated the cycle of inseminations with drug assistance for nine more months. It was now over two years into our journey, we remained childless and tried to focus on celebrating the blessings of our friends, some of whom were now on their path to their second child. Our dream home that we built was filled with disappointment, and we decided we needed a new endeavor to focus our efforts.

In hopes of rekindling a passion apart from our journey to parenthood, we decided to sell our home and begin the design process for a new home. Despite the distraction, we remained determined to have a child. The combination of keeping our fertility life a secret, dodging routine questions about a future pregnancy, and repeating the lie that the timing simply wasn't right was starting to take a toll on us and no distraction could fix our tiredness. Each month, our hopes would soar high only to come crashing down by the inevitable negative pregnancy test.

Something had to change.

It was time to give up our secret.

JOHNNY SIRPILLA

CHAPTER 3

Beyond Our Imagination

"Johnny and Susan ... doesn't your friends having babies want you to have one?"

"When you're ready and not so focused on your careers, you two will be amazing parents."

"I know that work is important but having kids is amazing."

"Someday you two will be ready for a family but don't rush it if you're not ready. You'll know when it is time."

General conversations with others were innocent but they had no idea about our secret, so without realizing it, they created some moments that began as awkward and ended as painful. They hadn't a clue of how badly we wanted a baby of our own.

We gave up our fight for secrecy. We finally opened up. Speaking openly with our closest friends, our parents, and my family about what we had endured over the past years was draining. Repeating the story brought us down, but the love and emotion we received in return provided hope and support. There was a sense of shame in letting down our facade of the career focused couple that appeared to have it all. Although our marriage remained strong and our love for each other even stronger, we felt a deep sense of failure on what really mattered ... creating a family.

Following the advice of our doctors, we began IVF (in-vitro fertilization). Susan's eggs would be produced with more drugs and then surgically removed from her ovaries and combined with my sperm to create an embryo in a petri dish. Not fully comprehending the church's belief against such medical procedures, we held true that God knew our hearts. Choosing to not fully explore the church's concerns, we told ourselves that with God's help and blessings, we would become parents and the miracle of that baby would be God's plan for us revealed.

When we met with the infertility specialist for our first consultation, we again had the hope that this was the next step necessary for the completion to our grand plan. Sitting at his desk, we noticed an ultrasound photo behind him and asked why it was on his board. He explained that it was an ultrasound of triplets. Our expressions told him that we would love to have multiples, but his reply gave a caution to the IVF process. He explained, "I keep the ultrasound image on my wall as a reminder to potential parents that triplets are not the desired outcome." He continued, "That's because the woman's body wasn't meant to carry three babies safely to term." We accepted this and knew our hearts would feel full with a single pregnancy. However, there was work to be done prior to that point, so our minds quickly abandoned those thoughts and we listened to his plan for us.

With adjustments to the drug dosage that Susan had been receiving, he stated that our goal was to produce 6-8 eggs and hope for fertilization in the 70% range. We followed the necessary steps, added in a few new drugs as prescribed, and prepared for our first cycle the next month.

Embracing our surrender to secrecy, we thought it would be nice to include our mothers with us at the hospital for Susan's egg retrieval. Inviting our loving mothers whose hearts were aching for their children just felt like the right thing to do. As Susan was taken away to surgery, I returned to the waiting area with my mom and mother-in-law.

My mom, Veronica, and her mom, Ella, hit it off from their first meeting and maintained a close friendship past what is required of in-laws. In fact, our parents socialized often without us. It felt natural to be flanked by these two-amazing women in the waiting area as the anxiety and worry began to flood my mind. I felt blessed with Susan's perseverance through the depth of what her mind, body and spirit had undergone for the last few years. I wanted both our mothers to see first-hand Susan's strength and share in my thankfulness for what she was willing to do for all of us.

As my mom would reflect years later, *"I think about all the doctor appointments and all that Susan went through physically.*

She never complained. She welcomed every opportunity to become a mother at any personal cost to herself. I could not have endured what she did. It was too much for one woman to endure."

As a sappy full-blooded Italian guy, I could practically feel the emotion and excitement of the day as I sat between our mothers. We had withheld our stress of the past several years from them, so with this final step in the infertility process, we wanted them to be able to experience everything with us. Looking back, oh, how I had wished that I really thought this through before we invited them to the egg retrieval surgery.

As I sat in the waiting area, my mother on my right and my mother-in-law on my left, (yes, the clarity of our seating arrangement remains etched in my mind twenty-eight years later) a nurse approached and said that it was time for me to provide my "contribution" to the invitro-fertilization process.

I froze.

Dear Lord, this could not be happening. What parenting book offers the protocol for excusing oneself from a set of mothers to knowingly "contribute?" Do I look them in the eyes and say I will be right back? Allow them to wish me luck? Offer up a half sympathetic smile and politely excuse myself?

Of course, there is no protocol for this situation because only an overly emotional Italian man like me would invite his mother and mother-in-law to their grandchildren's hopeful conception. In the back of my mind, I heard Susan's sound voice from just earlier that day questioning if it was a good idea to have our mothers present. But now wasn't the time to concede that her level-headed thinking was right, yet again.

I chose dignity (what little dignity I could scrape up in the situation) and rose from my seat without acknowledgment to them. As a man who felt the need to fill the silence in the room with unnecessary words, I was determined to remain quiet, block out my surroundings and leave our mothers in silence. My mother's face buried in a magazine was all the proof that I needed to know that this wasn't her proudest moment. Deciding on how to re-enter the waiting room was a problem that I wasn't ready to tackle at the moment. Off I go, and despite the pit in my stomach from an emotionally scarring experience, I had only one role to play on this day.

The nurse escorted me to a patient room, opened the door for me, and allowed me to walk in. The door shut behind me. I noticed a professional business briefcase on the examination table and sat in the chair waiting for further instruction. Thirty minutes later there is a knock on the door and a nurse asking, "Mr. Sirpilla, is everything okay?". I opened the door and explained to the nurse, "I'm fine. I'm simply waiting for the sterile cup to be provided."

"Everything that you need is in the briefcase, sir," she replied.

I'm not sure why but it never occurred to me to open the briefcase. It wasn't mine and I wasn't given instruction. I filled the awkward moment with a comment to the nurse on the other side of the door, "You're probably getting some clarity on why it's been hard for us to have a baby … my wife has been trying to make one with *me*." She was kind and sympathetically laughed with me to ease the tension.

My next thought raced to our mothers in the waiting room. They had to be wondering what was taking so long. But I certainly can't be thinking about our mothers now … those thoughts had to go … focus, Johnny, focus. Susan was under sedation, unconscious and in an operating room and she was *still* right … our mothers shouldn't have come.

As if there had not been enough signs that medical intervention to conceive was straying from our church's beliefs, I open the briefcase to receive yet another confirmation. The sterile cup I had been waiting for was accompanied by rubber gloves and several pornographic magazines. Everything in my body protested in revolt. "This just isn't how this is supposed to be!" I thought to myself in complete exasperation. "The love of my life was under anesthesia in surgery, and I'm somewhere else in the hospital with magazines that a happily married, committed husband should not have!"

I grabbed the sterile cup and gloves, closed the briefcase, and prayed for peace to come to me. Mission accomplished.

As I returned to our mothers in the waiting room, I simply said "I'm sorry about putting you in that position today. Let's return our focus to Susan, shall we?" They were both gracious, hugged me and no words were needed. I live by the motto that great laughs can cure even the most awkward of situations. Turn it into a funny story, and the scars will eventually heal.

Susan emerged from anesthesia in tears. The egg retrieval was very painful, as she had fallen in and out of consciousness and felt more of the procedure than expected. Her egg production was beyond what we had hoped for, and the doctors were able to extract 23 healthy and viable eggs. My over-achieving wife had far surpassed the goal of 6-8 and provided many IVF cycles of eggs if needed. They could have continued harvesting but Susan was feeling the needle being inserted over and over and the doctors saw her discomfort. Twenty-three was more than a win.

Forty-eight hours later, we returned to the hospital to see if fertilization was successful. Thankfully, we were greeted with news that the cells had continued to multiply, and we had healthy embryos for the transfer procedure.

Complicating our stress further, however, was the sudden death of my grandmother during this time. Susan and I had invited her over for my birthday dinner two weeks earlier, and we both noticed that she didn't seem like herself. After taking her home, we decided to go back and check on her a few hours later and realized that we needed to call an ambulance. She was diagnosed with a staph infection and died within a week.

Our large Italian family surrounded her at the hospital throughout her final week on earth as we formed a vigil for her. Susan and I used the vacant room next to her to administer the required injections to prepare for IVF. The evening of the egg retrieval was my grandmother's calling hours which Susan was not able to attend due to the pain she was feeling from the day. Needless to say, we were exhausted. After a much-needed night's rest, we were mindful that we had said goodbye to the matriarch of our family and held hope of a new Sirpilla life.

With the hopes of fertilizing 70% of the eggs, we were overwhelmed when we received the news that 95% of the eggs were fertilized. We were now parents of 22 embryos. Again, as we celebrated our seemingly successful results, we had no idea of the life-threatening challenge that we would face in the years ahead based on this decision. We were living in the moment, and we allowed our minds to quickly refocus on the next goal: implantation.

We knew from the initial meeting that pregnancy was not guaranteed through IVF. But we were on a good path so far and decided to keep the positive energy rolling. We were advised that implanting five embryos would put us in the best position to produce the long-awaited baby. The remaining embryos would be frozen for potentially needed future cycles. I held Susan's hand throughout the embryo transfer, and after several hours of her resting in the hospital bed, we were told that we could leave. We were told to return 14 days later for a pregnancy test. After all that it took to get to this point, I felt that we should have her stay in that bed and not move until delivery, but as I said, I can tend to be an anxious thinker.

We filled our minds with prayers for success and began the waiting game again. After years of practice, we knew the drill. We focused intensely on our work and looked for welcomed distractions everywhere. As a pharmaceutical sales representative, Susan busied herself with bringing medical samples to doctors' offices, providing lunches for the many doctor's offices she served and promoting her drugs. Our friends and family filled the waiting period with love and support until the fateful day came. We returned to the hospital for testing with positive thoughts as Susan had yet to start her period and we had yet to notice any of the all too familiar signs that "Aunt Flo" might be arriving.

Arriving at the IVF department we were greeted with kindness and shared anticipation. They gave us hope and told us to expect a call later that evening with the results. These were the days before cell phones so that meant waiting by the house phone and staring at it to ring. The phone rang, I answered and heard words that changed our lives. "Susan's pregnant and with a strong hCG (pregnancy hormone) count. It worked!" We received the proper cautions that IVF cycles may produce higher rates of miscarriage, but we needed the celebration and enjoyed the incredible feeling of good news.

We returned to the hospital an hour away every other day to ensure that Susan's hCG levels were increasing and at least doubling to show signs of a growing baby. As a numbers guy, I loved the numerical evidence and reassurance that things were headed in the right direction. Her numbers were high and aggressively growing. Praise God, our dream was becoming a reality.

We rejoiced in telling our family and friends the good news. In those moments of reveal, we were embraced and overwhelmed by the genuine excitement of loving family and friends, some of whom were brought to tears with the news.

Life presents us with so many beautiful moments to learn from others. So many times, while reflecting on the reaction we received, I ponder if I provided the depth of sincerity I received? Were my celebrations and expression of love significant enough to equal the intensity of others?

I love to take meaningful life moments and challenge myself to live and express to the level that I am capable of giving. Teachable moments surround us and it is upon us to soak them in so an experience isn't lost for growth. This was definitely a classroom session when I became a student of incredible teachers in life's biggest moments.

I concluded that in other's moments of celebration, I fell short of what I received and felt the need for personal growth stirring within me. It was effortless for Susan to be gracious and truly feel inner happiness by joyous news from others. Knowing that we were still on this journey together, I admired what she held so naturally within her and felt as though I needed to catch up to her in this regard.

CHAPTER 4

The Design of Angels

The fact that we were actually pregnant seemed surreal.

It was like winning *big* on game night.

But unbeknownst to us, much better than a game, we were about to win *the Mega Ball Lottery*!

The years of disappointment leading up to this point caused a delay in our full comprehension of the blessing that we were receiving. Thankfully, our years of infertility prepared us for the extent of medical intervention that was needed daily to ensure a successful pregnancy. To sustain the pregnancy, for three months I administered daily Progesterone injections to Susan. Each day, I massaged the area to make room for the drug as I slowly administered the jelly like substance into her. It was thick and difficult to get into her system.

As strange as it sounds, we became so accustomed to this routine that it was almost disappointing when the medication was no longer necessary because we felt that we were doing more than needed for the baby's safety.

JOHNNY SIRPILLA

We looked forward to our first ultrasound. We knew that we wouldn't be able to hear a heartbeat … it would be too soon. But we looked forward to seeing the physical proof that we were indeed pregnant.

But something important was about to change.

+ + +

Around this time, I had a short business trip, and when I returned home that evening, Susan told me that she had a surprise for me in our bedroom. Her smile was so beautiful as she grabbed my hand to lead me upstairs.

"What's going on?" I asked curiously, as we climbed the stairs hand in hand.

"I made a trip to the doctor's office earlier today," she replied. "I didn't feel well, so I wanted some reassurance that I was okay and that the baby was okay."

Immediately, my hands grew sweaty, my mouth dry and my mind raced about why she thought something was wrong. My heart rate quickly spiked. Even though recent tests had shown strong hCG levels, immediate worry, a consequence of years of infertility, had set in. She knew that's what I would be thinking so she reassured me as we approached our bedroom door. "Relax, Johnny, everything is okay…actually more than okay."

When I opened the door, I realized our lives had been changed forever.

On our bed sat three stuffed teddy bears. Each one was about eighteen inches tall, brown, furry, and dressed in traditional teddy bear style. It wasn't the individual bear that caught my attention, but the number grouped at the head of the bed. My eyes fixated on the *three* teddy bears as my heart continued to race. I could barely sputter out one word .... *triplets*?

The smile on her face filled the room, and our emotions overwhelmed us. Shock, disbelief, joy ... I felt it all. How could we possibly deserve such a blessing? She showed me an ultrasound picture with three individual sacs labeled A, B, and C. We laid on the bed and cried tears of joy as we tightly held onto those simple little teddy bears, symbolic of our immediate attachment to each baby. Our blessings were three-fold, and we held each other with gratitude.

Since we were living at my parent's home at the time (our house was being built), we grabbed the three teddy bears, sped down the stairs and excitedly shared the good news with my mom and dad. They were thrilled, of course. Especially my dad. My cousin and his wife had twins when I was seventeen --- I spent so much time with them and loved helping to care for them in the early months of their lives. They remain two of my most favorite people and my dad was so fascinated by the Sirpilla twins.

At the doctor's office that morning, it had been suggested to Susan that we not tell anybody that it was triplets—not just yet. However, we threw that counsel right out the window!

It was a Friday night, so naturally, we spent the entire weekend sharing the big news - many, many times over. How fun it was to share with our family and friends of the three babies that would soon fill our lives. It was like a good news tour to those closest to us. There was nothing more satisfying than being able to put smiles on so many faces that had loved us and supported us on our journey. In my mind, it was as if the prospect of three babies acted as a thank you for their constant support and a message to us that explained our infertility ... this was our destiny.

The question of whether we felt prepared to handle three babies at one time never crossed our minds. We felt that we were three times blessed and each thought that crossed our minds was laced with thankfulness.

After that glorious weekend, on Monday morning we called the hospital that performed the IVF procedure to tell them the good news. In the back of our minds, we remembered the doctor's caution that with triplets comes high risk pregnancies, but we were in celebration mode and our hearts were set on three. On the phone call, the doctor asked two critical questions that crushed our pure bliss.

"Did you see three sacs or three sacs with three heartbeats?"

Our answer to his question became the next cause for our anxious thoughts. It was still too early to hear a heartbeat, so we had the potential of triplets but not confirmation that we were actually pregnant with three babies. The six-week ultrasound posed as our next hurdle, and we counted down the days until we would hear three heartbeats to be sure that we were pregnant with triplets.

Next … *"You may want to consider "selective reduction" to secure a safer outcome."*

Shocked by the suggestion, without hesitation we disregarded it. We worked so hard to get pregnant. Abortion will not receive even the slightest consideration. We understood the medical perspective that he expressed by his comments, but no further discussion was needed.

Walking into the OB/GYN office two weeks later, our hearts were heavy as we prepared ourselves for the worst --- less than 3 heartbeats. Each step of the ultrasound felt as if the technician was purposely in slow motion. When she finally began the procedure, our hearts raced.

Baby A had a strong heartbeat!

Baby B had a strong heartbeat!

And yes, Baby C had a strong heartbeat!

This was really happening!

Within days, Susan began getting sick. Really sick. Not a normal pregnancy nauseous feeling but full-blown vomiting at least seven times a day. And it wasn't just in the morning, either. She felt it in the morning, throughout the entire day, and even at bedtime. As only Susan could, she powered through each day, working full time as a pharmaceutical sales representative. She was on the move daily, going in and out of doctors' offices, delivering medical samples, and hosting lunches. As needed, she would pull over to the side of the road to throw up and then resume her workday. It was not unusual for her to remove herself from presentations to get to the rest room. This became her new normal as the sickness continued week after week. Although we were hoping that she would be better for the Christmas holiday, she was in bed most of the time. She maintained a strong spirit and was happy to be there because she was pregnant. She didn't complain and graciously accepted the fact that a triplet pregnancy meant that there was three times the number of hormones. Many women feel sick during pregnancy, and she saw this as her turn. She lost about 15 pounds in the first trimester, despite every attempt to keep food down. At 5'8" and 130 pounds pre-pregnancy, she became very thin after the first trimester despite a growing belly of someone in their 5th or 6th month of pregnancy.

Looking back, I really was worried about Susan's health, but the worry was lost in my elation about the three babies. It was a mistake on my part for not pressing Susan to stop working and take it easy. Neither one of us were listening to her body and since she never even mentioned working less or complained at the end of the day, I went along with the plan to 'power through it.'

Early in the second trimester, she woke up and said, "It's over. I'm not sick anymore." And it was that simple, throwing up as a daily routine was over. As with most of our journey, as we set down one cross, there was another just around the corner. Fatigue became her new cross to carry. She was still working full time and in retrospect, pushing too hard. As a competitive athlete, she maintained a mindset that she must power through each day and do what needed to be done. Her body deserved better treatment, but we were young and naïve.

We were building a new house, both working full time, and Susan was growing our family inside of her! Despite the busy times and fatigue, we celebrated every day that we were soon to be a family of five! The time flew by quickly, and we shared the joys of pregnancy with three couples who were some of our closest friends. Each couple held-- and still holds to this day-- a special place in our hearts. One couple was due about two months before us with their second baby, and the other two couples were due within a week or so of our due date. On top of this, one couple approached the birth of their third, and my cousin and his wife were expecting their first. Four Sirpilla babies were coming at the same time, along with two other built in best friends and we all felt the magic of the times ahead.

+ + +

It was important to us to not find out the sexes of the babies, so we could be surprised at delivery. We faced the temptation to ask at weekly ultrasounds to ensure each baby was growing as they should, but we reminded the ultrasound technician at the beginning of each session, "Remember, no reference to gender, please. Just refer to them as Baby A, B or C. And no pronouns allowed."

Not knowing if we were going to have three girls, three boys, or a mix of two and one, we decided that we would be gender neutral with the nursery. We love being different in our interior design work so this was a chance to introduce this theme in an important space.

We like to be creative, and we knew we didn't want the 'normal' nursery theme of bears or trains or something of that nature. Both of us holding our faith and spirituality close throughout our entire journey, we chose cherub angels as the theme for the nursery. Angels are a big part of our spiritual connection. One example: My grandmother died while we were involved in IVF and I can recall lighting a votive candle in an angel candleholder, asking her for prayers for us.

We view angels as more than cuddly little babies with halos and wings. Consider this quote from St. Thomas Aquinas:

"An angel can illumine the thought and mind of man by strengthening the power of vision and by bringing within his reach some truth which the angel himself contemplates."

And I love this beautiful Blessing:

"Angels around us, angels beside us, angels within us.
Angels are watching over you when times are good or stressed.
Their wings wrap gently around you,
Whispering you are loved and blessed."

Yes, angels are important to us.

I really could not have imagined a more exciting time in our lives. Using our collective creative sides to design and build our second home, we ensured the nursery was large enough for three cribs. We bought three of everything and found joy in the creativity of designing the nursery. We decided to paint the vaulted ceiling with soft blue clouds and adorned with paintings of cherub angels, allowing each baby a perfect view of the heavenly sky. When the artist completed her painting, Susan and I sat for hours in the nursery gazing upwards.

Three of everything.

This was going to be a very happy home.

The inspiration for the angel-themed nursery

Our mothers, Ella O'Brien and Veronica Sirpilla

JOHNNY SIRPILLA

CHAPTER 5

Footprints in the Sand

Valentine's Day 1995 was a sweet night. We were together, knowing that this was the last Valentine's Day that it would just be the two of us. We loved the fact that the future holidays would include a family of five. As much as we were in love with each other, we were more in love with our new family and the life that was ahead of us.

The following evening after work was like any other. We rested after a busy day and watched TV together. However, when Susan got up from her chair, she noticed that she was soaking wet. We weren't sure what had happened, but we knew that she had to get to the hospital immediately. Our first thought and worst fear was that her water had broken for one of the babies, even though it was far too early for delivery, and she hadn't felt any contractions. As we were in a full panic, my mom had just pulled in the driveway. My mom is the exact person you would want on your side in a traumatic situation, and she took command by driving us to the hospital, offering reassurance the whole way to keep us both calm.

We were taken straight to labor and delivery, our worst fear revealing itself. Baby A's water had broken. The baby was still alive with a trace amount of amniotic fluid, and Baby's B and C remained unharmed and content in their individual amniotic sacs. Susan was admitted and placed on bed rest as a host of medical professionals surrounded us with support. Her bed was placed in Trendelenburg position with her head level below her feet to take pressure off her cervix. It was a waiting game from ultrasound to ultrasound. The stress was unbelievable. With each ultrasound and heartbeat check we were praying that Baby A was still alive. Thankfully, day after day, Baby A survived.

There was serious concern for Susan's health, and the chance of infection increased alongside the toll of the pregnancy on her body. With all four lives at risk, there were discussions of attempting a partial delivery, a procedure our local hospital had not previously attempted. The thought was to deliver Baby A and quickly close her cervix, allowing Baby B and C to remain in utero. There was also discussion of transporting Susan to the Cleveland Clinic an hour away, but again the risks of transportation were at the forefront of conversation. We couldn't imagine making the decision to sacrifice one baby for the lives of the other two. It did not even seem real to be having those discussions, but they were necessary. We chose to continue the course of waiting and felt blessed that labor and contractions had never been a factor.

Baby A was fighting and miraculously still alive. We couldn't give up on this sweet soul and sacrifice his or her life to protect the others.

We started the eighth day in our hospital stay, February 22, 1995, just as the others. We completed our morning prayers and read aloud a beautiful prayer for our children, one that was becoming quickly committed to memory. We recited the prayer many times daily with our family and friends who surrounded and supported us around the clock.

Dear God,

There are no words for the depth of my love for these children.

I pray for their care and their protection.

I surrender them into Your hands.

Please, dear God, send Your angels to bless and surround them always.

May they be protected from the darkness of our times.

May they always see You at the center of their lives.

May their hearts grow strong,

To love You and serve You.

I surrender, dear God, my parenthood to You.

Make me the parent You want me to be.

Show me how to love most patiently, to be there for them most fully,

To understand profoundly who they are and what they need.

May this family be a blessing unto them now and forever.

May they learn here values and principles of love and righteousness.

May they learn from me kindness.
May they learn from me strength.
May they learn from me lessons of power:
That they have it and
Must surrender it to You, to be used for Your purposes
throughout their life
For thus You shall be gladdened,
And thus shall they be free,
To live most fully and love most deeply.
Amen.

The morning ultrasound showed that Baby A continued to remain healthy with a strong heartbeat, and Baby's B & C were comfortably growing in their respective amniotic sacs, hopefully unaware of the trauma that had been going on in their world. Each baby had grown over the past week, so we felt positive that today was going to be a good day.

Around lunch time, Susan began to develop a fever, a signal of an infection that would put all four lives at risk once again. The fever was soon followed by contractions and panicked medical discussions among doctors brought the reality of our worst fear to light. With the confirmation that Susan had an infection, delaying labor was no longer an option. We faced a choice that would affect the rest of our lives. With assistance, our children could potentially live in neo-natal intensive care for days or even a few weeks. Or we could choose to keep them with us, in our arms, for as long as they lived naturally. Our first thought was the pain they may feel with injections and attempts to keep them alive in intensive care. We needed a few more weeks in utero to give them a fighting chance, and we appreciated the honesty of the doctors and nurses as they counseled us, tears welling in their eyes. We had become friends with the nurses and doctors and knew their words to us were medically sound and delivered with care. We formed an incredibly close friendship with Dr. Prab Gill, which continues today, and his impact in our lives reached far beyond this tragic day.

Labor was progressing slowly and due to the infection, Susan was not able to receive any pain medication. During the eight hours of labor, our closest friends and family remained by our side. One by one and all aware of the risk Susan was facing, they came into the delivery room to share their love and tears of disbelief. The prayers that filled the private waiting room from our family were intense to say the least. Prayers for Susan's life, prayers for the babies, prayers for my strength, and prayers for our own parents were critical and carried us through the treacherous hours. In the eye of the storm, I felt horrible for our parents. Watching their worry and grief while they tried to be strong for us was almost more than I could handle.

In the last hour, Susan and I sat alone in the room as doctors and nurses shuffled in and out to check on her. She was breathing through the pain, and we shook in fear of what was ahead of us. Susan's temperature and infection continued to elevate, and we talked through the reasons why we would keep the babies with us until their natural death. It seemed as though each time that we settled on a decision, hope that they might survive would overtake us. Then the crushing reality of the medical professionals' comments would return to the forefront of our minds. We decided that we wanted their time on earth to be as peaceful and pain free as possible, their entire lives spent cradled in our arms.

With one final check, we were told it was time to start pushing. It all just seemed so counterintuitive. She had been warding off labor for over a week, and now it was time to engage in it. At this same time, something happened. Something beautiful and greater than us. Our tears stopped as we locked eyes with each other and without a spoken word, our spirits aligned. We both felt it. We were not alone. Baby A was born, and we had our first son. Immediately, I was able to hold him and meet our son. I brought him to Susan's view, and together we admired the beauty of God's creation. He was terribly bruised from not having the protection of an amniotic sac and enduring the innocent kicks of his siblings. His face was swollen from the bruising, but he looked like a little warrior hanging on to life so he could meet his parents. As we marveled at him, joy overtook us. Both of us. Pure joy.

The calmness that settled over the room was interrupted by a gentle voice from the doctor telling Susan that it was time to start pushing again for our next baby. Our daughter came out beautifully unmarked with a sense of sweetness about her that felt different than her warrior brother. Now with my son and daughter in my arms and lying beside Susan, we felt a bliss that prepared us to meet our next baby.

With the easiest push yet, our third child was born, and our family was united. Susan's work was done with the delivery, and she could now embrace each baby. Mindfully aware that we both wanted as much time as possible with each baby, I gently laid our oldest son on her chest to make room in my arms for our second son. There were no tears, only vibrant smiles. We were a blessed family of five, knowing our lifetime together belonged to this hospital room. We were joyful and grateful for the love that we felt. The connection to each baby sustained us as we looked at each other knowing, somehow knowing, that we needed to soak up each movement they made and breathe with them as that they took their remaining breaths.

There was a peace in the room, and we were a happy and complete family. With each gentle breath of our sons and daughter, we were overwhelmed with gratefulness. Our first son, Nicholas O'Brien, was the first to slow his movements and take his last breath. We watched him let go of his bruised body and enter the gates of heaven. We felt a change, and we accepted it. Our daughter Mary Susan soon followed Nicholas but prior to taking her last breath, she raised her left arm up to her face and tucked her left wrist under her chin to rest her head on it. Soon after, she was gone. While still holding Nicholas and Mary, our attention turned to Peter Anthony. For a moment we looked at him with hope that he might just hang on. But we knew better. Peter was a bit slimmer than Nicholas, likely due to the bruising and swelling that Nicholas sustained, but he had a calm about him that made him feel different. Peter took his last breaths and joined his brother and sister in heaven.

Susan and I held them, prayed over them, and passed them back and forth to each other, so we could have one on one time with them. Unfortunately, Susan had to be taken to surgery because Peter's placenta remained in her, and a new worry hit us—how Susan's body would uphold during surgery after undergoing so much trauma during birth. The goodbye was heartbreaking as she was wheeled out of the room, and she tearfully said goodbye to Nicholas, Mary, and Peter. Again, she was emotionally and physically enduring so much. How much more could she take? I was emotionally hitting a wall and had not even undergone the physical pain that had been Susan's new normal throughout our journey.

As a proud father, I could think of only one thing to do: introduce our babies to our family. One by one, I brought them out to greet the people we loved most so they could have their connection with Nicholas, Mary, and Peter. I can vividly remember feeling such happiness and pride without any weight of the sorrow that would hit me later. I observed the reactions from others, each unique and ranging from tears to sobs, to even running in the other direction with emotion. While I was aware of the reactions, I wasn't feeling the same. This poem by Mary Fishback Powers best describes how Susan and I felt during the time that Nicolas, Mary, and Peter were alive and during their passing. While we didn't fully comprehend it at the time, our hearts felt it. This divine intervention laid the foundation for us to sustain what had yet to unfold.

Footprints in the Sand

One night I dreamed a dream.
As I was walking along the beach with my Lord.
Across the dark sky flashed scenes from my life.
For each scene, I noticed two sets of footprints in the sand,
One belonging to me and one to my Lord.
After the last scene of my life flashed before me,
I looked back at the footprints in the sand.
I noticed that at many times along the path of my life,
especially at the very lowest and saddest times,
there was only one set of footprints.
This really troubled me, so I asked the Lord about it.
"Lord, you said once I decided to follow you,
You'd walk with me all the way.
But I noticed that during the saddest and most troublesome
times of my life,
there was only one set of footprints.
I don't understand why, when I needed You the most, You
would leave me."
He whispered, "My precious child, I love you and will never
leave you
Never, ever, during your trials and testings.
When you saw only one set of footprints,
It was then that I carried you."

CHAPTER 6

Our Guardian Angels

For several hours while Susan was in surgery, I had the blessing of remaining in the delivery room with Nicholas, Mary, and Peter. Our family and friends joined together while we collectively prayed for Susan's surgery and the souls of our triplets. With heavy hearts, everyone searched for the right words to make some sense of the past three years of constant struggle and quite simply what had just happened.

My initial thought was simple. How do I comprehend the magnitude of the loss that we just suffered? How do we possibly move forward from here? My thoughts remained frozen there until one of the nurses entered the room with a sobering question. "What funeral home will you be using? We will call them to pick up the babies."

Ugh ... We now faced a new reality: a funeral to plan with a scheduled move into our new home approaching in the next two days. Susan was going to be hospitalized for several more days, and I couldn't leave her side. I'm not saying that I couldn't leave her out of a gesture to be a good husband, but

I actually needed to be with her. She was feeling what I was feeling-- that our brief time as a family of five was gone, and it is just the two of us again. I needed her. It was that simple.

We were fortunate that our mothers were very close friends. They loved each other and could share in the experience of two mothers grieving. Grief for what their children were experiencing and grief for the loss of their grandchildren. It truly broke us to watch their pain. They were so loving and good. They deserved to be holding Nicholas, Mary, and Peter and showering them with love and instead, they said to us, "Let us plan the funeral and select the gravesite." They went on to say, "We just can't bear to have you two go through those details and we want to plan the only sacrament our grandchildren will receive in the Catholic church."

It was a tremendous help, yet it pained me to know that they were taking these steps for us as I remained with Susan in the hospital. Our only request was one casket, so Nicholas, Mary, and Peter could always remain together as they had been throughout their entire lives.

Infant death can be misunderstood by many, and there may not be a generally accepted "standard" for funeral services. To us, it was simple. The value and impact of our children's lives was not going to be measured by the span of time between their birth and death certificates. There would be only one public celebration in their lifetime. We appreciated the opportunity to see as many people as possible at the calling hours, so that our future interactions were not entirely steeped in sorrow of the birth and passing of our children.

Our friends and family were busy in those days following. They worked tirelessly so that when we arrived in our new home on Saturday from the hospital, everything was in its place. We didn't ask them for their help—they just did it! The three were born on a Wednesday and our house was completed two days later on Friday. The movers were already booked to deliver our furniture on that day, so our friends and family took over and made sure that it happened in an efficient and orderly procedure.

Our clothes were organized in our closets, the kitchen was perfectly stocked, and every room was beautifully appointed with artwork on the walls and personal pictures set out throughout the rooms. My sister, Laura, who was my partner in our clothing and furniture store threw herself into this project like no other. She couldn't do much to ease our pain, but she certainly could make our home beautiful and she would work around the clock to get that accomplished. Susan would come home the next day (Saturday) and the funeral would be two days later on Monday.

My sisters were in overdrive as they tried to explain to their own young children the loss of their cousins, all the while remaining by our sides. Our mothers planned the funeral for Monday with every detail in order. We were being taught through the kindness of others how to ease other's pain. Their incredible gestures made all the difference, and we tried to be mindful and grateful for them.

On Sunday evening before the calling hours and funeral the following morning, we received a knock on the door. It was a couple that we knew as acquaintances from our previous neighborhood, so their visit was a complete surprise to us. "We apologize for coming over during such a difficult time," they spoke tenderly, "but we need some time with you prior to the funeral and before too much time had passed."

I wasn't exactly sure what this visit was all about, but we invited them in to join us. As we sat down together, without any other small talk, they began explaining their visit. "We had a baby that passed away about twenty years ago. We learned a great deal from that experience. One thing we learned was the large percentage of couples who divorce after the loss of a child." They paused for a moment to allow that sobering statistic to settle in.

Leaning closer to us, they went on. "It's important for you to grieve together while knowing that each of you may grieve differently than the other." They continued, "There will be days when one of you is up and the other is down. You need to expect this and be patient with each other. You cannot let frustration with each other come between you."

"Thank you," was all we could say in response.

We were so grateful for their wise counsel. As it turned out, they were not only correct in sharing their wisdom through their own experience, but it taught us to pay it forward to others. Although it was too early to comprehend, their visit set the foundation for clarity and purpose that we would later need to survive.

+ + +

I can remember the details of the funeral as if our life was in slow motion. I believe this allowed me to capture moments so that they could be imprinted on my heart and mind in the future. It began with the ride in the limousine to St. John's Cathedral. We sat speechless, holding hands, and preparing for what was about to transpire. With memories of saying hello to our babies so fresh in our mind, we were forced to say our final goodbye.

I couldn't help but think how strange it seemed as I saw other people driving by, going about their day, without any acknowledgement of how our world was crumbling. It was just another day to so many, but to us, it was a tragic ending to years of hope and faith that left us motionless. I knew instinctively that I needed to remember these thoughts, because many days in the future, I would need to recall and share this experience to empathize with others' struggles.

Our mothers had each detail beautifully planned for the only sacrament in the Catholic church that Nicholas, Mary, and Peter would receive. With a closed casket, we chose to frame their handprints and footprints so we could share a tiny glimpse of our babies.

Susan was not able to stand during the calling hours, yet we were blessed for several hours to receive sympathies from our friends that attended the funeral mass. Post-delivery, her body was naturally preparing for her time as a mother to three babies. She continued to produce breast milk even though we had bound her chest with bandages to suppress the production. She was uncomfortable, emotional, and physically exhausted. As I looked at her sitting beside the casket, I continued to pray for strength. I wanted to hear every word of our friends, so I could use it as nourishment for my heart and soul to lead us to brighter days.

Knowing the funeral mass would be more than our family members could bear to actively participate, we asked my four closest friends to serve as pallbearers, our dear friends to provide the readings, cousins to offer the intentions, and another dear friend to read a letter of thanks from Susan and me.

My dad performed the eulogy. The thought that he was put in a position to eulogize his grandchildren still saddens me to this day. He gave the eulogy with his own style, open with his tears and speaking from his heart. One line has stuck with me all these years:

"Nicholas, Mary and Peter went from their mother and fathers' arms to our heavenly Father's arms, and there is something really beautiful about that."

Again, I knew these words would help me to move past the horrific pain and sadness I was experiencing. There is something so true about the innocence and purity of that statement that truly is beautiful. I registered that in the back of my mind and held on tightly, because the rest of my mind was swirling with an overload of thoughts, feelings and even confusion.

Why confusion? This isn't confusing. It is a tragedy, and my core feelings should simply be of sadness and disbelief. Our lives have been permanently altered for the worse. We will never be the same, never feel complete and healed from this, and we are failing at what is most important in our lives: creating a family. Yet something just felt like I really needed to think about the words of my father. I refocused my attention on the mass, knowing we still had to deal with the burial. One step at a time. As hard as funerals can be, I didn't want it to end. When it ended, we could not stand beside the casket and have that physical closeness to them anymore.

Leaving the church was more than we could take, knowing that we are going to take them to their final resting place. After this, we would be expected to move on and return to our lives in whatever form it was to take. Being an active thinker as I have said before, I thought about the importance of remembering this day, because it was the only public day that we would have as a family. I couldn't handle the thought of forgetting the day, so I hired a videographer to film the funeral. I didn't know if I would ever want to watch it, but I knew I didn't want to live with regret. I thought that maybe someday, if we ever had more children, they might want to see the tribute to their older brothers and sister, the love received by their parents, and the impact their siblings had on our family and community.

I have watched the funeral video over the years to reconnect to that time. The videographer was discreet in their filming, so no one really realized that they were there. The video ends after the graveside service with Susan and I sitting in front of the casket. In the final moments, everyone took a rose that was draped over the casket and took it with them as they left ... carrying a sign of our babies with them. They quietly filed out of the tented area, so we could be alone with our babies one last time. We sat quietly, cried, and said our goodbyes. We made promises to them that we have always kept. We will not forget them. We will not move on as if they weren't a critical part of our lives. And most importantly, we asked them to serve as guardian angels over us and their future siblings. If God's plan was to bless us again with another opportunity to be parents, we knew from our experience so far that there are no promises that it would be easy, and we needed our guardian angels.

Suddenly, we realized our decision to decorate with angels as the theme of their nursery carried a new meaning. Nicholas, Mary, and Peter were actually those angels painted in the clouds, soaring above the empty nursery in our new home.

Perhaps now you can understand more fully why angels are so very important to us.

Nicholas, Mary, and Peter Sirpilla remain together for eternity in their shared casket

Johnny and Susan's final goodbye to Nicholas, Mary, and Peter

CHAPTER 7

Why Not Us?

We all know that bad things happen to good people. Much has been written on the subject. As a matter of fact, there are two incredible books with similar titles that address that topic very well. One is titled *Why Do Bad Things Happen to Good People*, written by David Arnold and the other, *When Bad Things Happen to Good People* is by Harold Kushner.

Kushner is helpful when he writes: "*We can't pray that God make our lives free of problems; this won't happen, and it is probably just as well. We can't ask Him to make us and those we love immune to diseases, because He can't do that. We can't ask Him to weave a magic spell around us so that bad things will only happen to other people, and never to us.*

People who pray for miracles usually don't get miracles, any more than children who pray for bicycles, good grades, or good boyfriends get them as a result of praying. But people who pray for courage, for strength to bear the unbearable, for the grace to remember what they have left instead of what they have lost, very often find their prayer answered."

Courage, strength, grace—all good things that come from the bad.

For some people, when they struggle, they find themselves asking, "*Why me?*" It is such a common phrase. People would come up to me and say, "You're probably wondering *why me?*"

My answer to that was ALWAYS …. "No … I never ask '*why me?*'" It just seemed so natural to say the opposite--*why not me?* My mind and heart would go there quickly. It just seemed more logical.

Living in a world with so much tragedy, so much misfortune, and countless injustices, I find it illogical to think that I should have the privilege to be excluded from the trauma. While I believe that each one of us is subject to trauma in this world, I feel lucky that Susan and I both indulged in our share of blessings prior to battling infertility, the passing of Nicholas, Mary, and Peter and all that went with it. We viewed our challenge as our cross to bear in life. Both of our childhoods were steeped in stability and cultivated a sense of mindfulness about the misfortunes we were lucky enough to avoid. I appreciate that Susan and I shared in this mindset and upbringing, choosing to spend more time in the "Why not us?" train of thought and appreciating each individual blessing as its own. God knew we needed all our energy to handle the life ahead of us.

+ + +

We left Canton with my parents the day after the funeral to have some quiet time in Florida. Our thought was that Susan's body could heal and rest. We were painfully aware of the impact that the stress of the previous weeks (and years) had taken on her body and had the hopes of finding some sort of calm and acceptance. While it turned out that sunshine and sand could only go so far in dealing with our sadness, we needed the time to process our next steps. I know this sounds crazy. It was much too soon to think about what is next for us, but timing required we address three particular issues that would require some strategy on our part.

First, three couples we held close to our hearts were pregnant, and we knew we needed to be there for them at their deliveries.

The first delivery was about 10 days after the funeral, so we strategized a method to ensure that we were emotionally strong enough to be present for them in their time of celebration. Showing them genuine excitement and joy without any hint at our depressed state of mind was the only way in which we could adequately be present for them at the hospital. Because they provided such a constant source of strength for us in our sadness, we knew deep in our hearts that they deserved the reciprocal level of support in their celebration.

There was never a question of whether we would be able to go. We were already godparents to their son, and in this time, we needed to completely immerse ourselves in the happiness surrounding the birth of their new daughter. We realized through our time away that their happiness does not have to be joined with ours or serve as a connecting point to our pain. This train of thought assisted us in separating the two distinct events, working hard to internalize their joy without veering towards any negative thoughts of comparison. We promised to one another we would be present for others, without falling into self-pity. We continually monitored our thoughts, ensuring that we spent little to no time in a space of selfishness. We already knew how we felt. We were broken, and we wouldn't wish this type of brokenness on any other being. Thinking in that frame served no one. Even though the pain was fresh and new to us, their friendship was longstanding and deserved our hearts joined with theirs as their family grew.

So again, why not us? Feeling slightly steadier and resolute in our intentions, we flew home a day before the scheduled C-section of their daughter. Walking into the exact same labor and delivery unit, we found strength in looking to one another as a visual reminder of our private pact to positivity. This was not about us. Our preparation paid off; it was their time of celebration, and we successfully played our part in facilitating joy.

As if this birth didn't take strength enough, we would need to repeat this process two more times in the next two months. We fought off the feelings of comparison and were mindful to be present for them as they had been for us. I would not say that the deliveries were by any stretch of the imagination easy for us, in fact, after a cheerful visit to the hospital for the next birth, the weight of the situation caught up with Susan. We gathered strength as we entered the hospital, felt the love and joy of meeting an important new baby in our lives, but when we left the hospital room, Susan fell to the ground in the hallway. She literally collapsed as soon as we were out of site from our cousins and their new baby. The emotional toll had caught up to her and while she kept it together to enjoy our visit, her spirit understandably hit a breaking point. Our clear mindsets and preparation had succeeded in being there for our dear friends and family but it was now time to turn again to Barb's cognitive behavioral therapy and refresh so we could move forward.

We derived our strength from a strong mental plan and intentional prayer for selflessness. We did not entirely suppress the flood of emotions each time we witnessed the beautiful births, but we knew the time and place to express these feelings. Surprisingly, selflessly immersing ourselves in the celebrations and sharing in happiness of our friends was the best remedy we could have asked for in our time of mourning.

+ + +

Once our emotions were in check, we shifted down our to do list. Getting our personal lives on solid ground did not appear to be enough. My emotions followed me throughout the day; from waking up, to the cemetery, and to work. This is when I realized that there wasn't a work/life balance...

there was just *life*. Next up: the culture at my business, Sirpilla RV Center.

In a very reflective state, I began to realize the ways I had permitted a toxic culture at work. Throughout my time as a second-generation business owner, my dad often reminded me that two out of three second-generation businesses fail. A little pressure? Maybe, yet it was a reality, and he only wanted the best for the company he built from the ground up. Our company, 36 years old at the time-- older than me—was honored to be supported by many committed employees that had clocked their entire career at Sirpilla RV Center. Longevity and intracompany growth opportunities served as the main pillars to the community we created. However, beneath the pretty surface, an underlying tone of negativity and criticism emanated from our corporate culture, creating anxiety as I thought about returning to work.

I felt mentally fragile and recognized this mental state was not apt to handle the type of culture I would soon have to return to at the office. I knew I was not stable enough, nor should I ever be, to tolerate this type of behavior or perform as an effective leader in this functioning yet dysfunctional environment. While I wished I could implement this change immediately, I was aware that work cultures do not change automatically. I would need to be strategic and fair to our loyal employees as I developed a plan.

Sirpilla RV took pride in its devoted and trustworthy employees, but tension rooted in criticism, blame, and divisiveness had settled over the work force. Water cooler discussions and casual conversations of problems were far more frequent in the workplace than formal and strategic meetings. On top of this, there seemed to be a notion of pleasure felt by one team when another team stumbled. Teams would rejoice in the opportunity to point out the errors that led to customer disappointment while seeming to miss their own flaws that contributed to customer service below our standards.

While I had a sense of this environment before the triplet's death, our recent experiences allowed me to return to work with a fresh perspective and an unwillingness to tolerate any form of viciousness in a professional setting. In losing the triplets, I discovered a new sense of responsibility as an employer. I now understood that the type of situation Susan and I had just journeyed together outside of our work lives wasn't unique to my 70 employees. I realized that I had let our workforce down by failing to provide a more supportive work culture, an environment that would carry them throughout the day and allow them to return to their families at their best.

The bottom line was simple-- I could feel the tension building in my chest as I thought about returning to the company on which I prided my career. This was a problem. Yet, I was granted the opportunity to band the company together, bring recreation to families, and gain an insider's glimpse into the pain that many of our employees carried to work on a daily basis.

Within a few weeks, I implemented a program called Forward Focus, which would serve as the behavioral foundation of our culture. I gathered the employees together in several group meetings to explain the reasons a change was necessary. I focused on the benefits that this program would have in our work relationships. Rather than allowing employees to nod along without tangible progress, I set a timetable for each employee, detailing the leeway time allowed for them to fully understand and embrace the program. I explained that the change to workplace behaviors was technically optional in the present moment. At the same time, I explicitly noted to them that I would reassess employment at the completion of Forward Focus.

Over the next year, I conducted a series of seminars that outlined what it would look like to work in a Forward Focus culture and how current tendencies would need to change to comply. In addition to fostering greater awareness of inflammatory dialogue patterns, I began messaging *Chicken Soup for the Soul* stories on the cover page of our twice monthly newsletter. Feel good stories were the headline news! My intention was not only to inspire our employees, but also to remind the workforce that they are more than capable of choosing to re-frame difficult situations in their lives.

In Forward Focus, we find solutions and answers to our challenges. We focus on our strengths, the power of collaboration, and what we genuinely like about ourselves and each other. From the beginning of Forward Focus, it was made clear that the repetition of conversations about one another's deficiencies in their work and problems without a clear intention to find solutions was not acceptable dialogue. We did not ignore problems and areas of improvement, but we focused time and energy into figuring out the best manner of approach. We approached each area of concern with an eye out for a solution.

We focused on the talents already in the dealership that could assist in overcoming a challenge and the ways in which we could work collaboratively to improve situations. I refused to ignore reality. In some cases, we needed to outsource talent, but the decisions to do so were always collaborative among current employees and just one facet of the solution.

Breaking old habits was challenging but I knew that I could not work in an environment that didn't align with this model. I restrained myself from forcing certain people to change, especially those who genuinely didn't believe Forward Focus would succeed. The goal was simple:

To foster an uplifting environment that allowed employees to feel valued and appreciated and in turn, deliver exceptional customer service.

I hoped that their successes throughout the day would lead them to return home to their families energized after a good day's work. At its core, the program was intended to promote a healthy work-life balance and allow the employee to return energized to their most important role—their role as a mother, father, wife, husband, grandparent, caretaker, or friend. As I reflected about how far work can reach beyond the office and subsequently, the toll that a negative work culture can take on relationships, I became sick with guilt. I vowed to myself I would end this negativity to the best of my ability at Sirpilla RV. The plan increased opportunities for private discussions and assistance for those willing to accept the culture. With the intricacies of Forward Focus fresh in the employees' minds, I explicitly reminded them that at the end of one year, it would be a joint decision whether they would retain their position.

Without apology, I was firm with my commitment to the program. It may not have initially been a culture that everyone felt was necessary or worked in their favor, but I consistently reminded our employees that a feeling of discomfort was okay. At the end of the year, I removed two employees from the company. By many standards, they were valuable based on their production, industry knowledge and experience. However, they stunted the growth of the community and in certain ways, acted as a cancer stirring other's negativity.

The following year sales and profitability were the highest in company history. This trend continued year after year with growth from the top line to the bottom line. The correlation between the culture and the customer experience was clear and direct.

While these statistics were entirely satisfying, what encouraged me the most about the change was the flood of letters that I received from family members of our employees. Letter after letter came in, all sharing one consistent theme:

their family member was coming home happier each day after work, and it was positively impacting their home life. Some letters spoke directly to our program with their thanks. Others simply said something along the lines of, "I don't know what is happening at work, but thank you. There is a renewed happiness and respect in our home that was missing." As it turns out, kindness transpires and turns out to be good business on many levels.

Jumping ahead 8 years, I believe this cultural foundation transformed my business which led to a career changing opportunity when I was one of the initial acquisitions by Camping World in 2003. Although I never had plans to sell Sirpilla RV, especially at the age of 36, I saw an opportunity to make an imprint on the RV industry as my father and extended family did over the previous 40+ years. The national stage in the formation of the first RV dealership roll up model was the place I needed to be in this time of my career. Over the next 14 years, I served as President of Camping World and ultimately Chief Business Development Officer of the parent company, Camping World and Good Sam. I retired in 2017, after a successful IPO which took place on my 50th birthday. Serving as a key executive in a company with over $4 billion in revenue, over 10,000 employees, and several hundred locations was an experience of a lifetime. I'm forever grateful for the ways in which that experience further shaped the leader and man that I need to be for others. More importantly, the journey shared in this book gave me clarity for the character I needed to display, the integrity I demanded to uphold, and the leader I needed to be for the national stage and in the investment work that I'm doing today in my family office and numerous board seats.

I have a lot more to say about the responsibility one holds, beyond their defined scope of work, when they accept the title of manager, supervisor, VP or President—so much more that I am seriously considering a follow up book to this one exclusively focusing on that topic. Stay tuned.

+ + +

Third: the re-model of our family. We had seventeen frozen embryos at the clinic, and our desire to parent had not diminished after the death of Nicholas, Mary, and Peter. Despite having succeeded in giving birth at its simplest form, we felt so much worse than we had as an infertility couple. We now held on to a new layer of stress in our family planning. We spent a substantial amount of time at the cemetery to be physically close to our babies. While we realized that this wasn't necessarily a healthy practice in our mourning, it was a place that we both found comfort.

While we were still in a state of mourning, as soon as the doctors felt that Susan's body was ready, we embraced the opportunity for another embryo transfer. Approximately four months later, we returned to the clinic with confidence and optimism that the worst had to be behind us. We began the injections to medically prepare Susan's body for the embryos and completed the transfer. Just like that, once again we were in the two-week waiting game. This time, however, we had some experience behind us. Returning to the hospital for the subsequent blood work, we were embraced with genuine kindness from the doctors and nurses that helped us conceive Nicholas, Mary, and Peter. They were in our corner, giving us a sense of comfort rather than mourning when we walked into the hospital. Now old pros at the process, we knew by heart what to hope for in the blood test results and the desired hCG hormone level for each visit. The blood test came back positive with strong hCG levels, meaning there was another possibility for multiples.

We were pregnant again, and back on the path to creating our family.

The hCG levels were high and doubling every other day. The sickness began for Susan quickly, so we were not surprised to learn that we were expecting twins. A sense of relief rushed over us when we heard the news, because we had heard countless times that the complication levels are exponentially different between two and three babies. We clung to this reassurance and good news, trying at every turn to reduce the fears that we faced with another pregnancy. The daily progesterone injections began and before we knew it, we were back in our routine. The angel themed nursery was a little easier to walk by as a pregnant couple, and we began hoping for our future again. Weekly visits to our OB/GYN office provided confirmation that heartbeats were strong, and our babies were growing.

About eight weeks into the pregnancy, Susan began bleeding. We immediately rushed to the hospital, fully expecting that she had miscarried the twins. The ultrasound revealed that one baby was in fact miscarried, but Susan was still pregnant with the other baby. We felt sad, but also a sense of appreciation that one baby survived. We left the hospital counting our blessings. The risks associated with a twin pregnancy dissipated from our mind, and we rationalized our way through the miscarriage. Our hope prevailed.

The following weeks continued with sickness for Susan. We were always told that extended sickness meant the hormones were high, indicating a healthy pregnancy. In comparison to the sickness Susan felt carrying the triplets, she felt thankful to be sick at a more manageable level. Her selflessness continued to amaze me at every turn and with each hurdle, I stood beside her in awe of her physical and mental stamina. Susan adopted nearly all the principles that Barb taught us throughout the course of this time.

We returned weekly for ultrasounds, each week our anxieties heightened by the day until, yet another image of our baby quelled our worries. Unfortunately, the relief only lasted an hour or two after reassurance, so our insecurities remained high in between appointments. As we approached week 12, our fears slightly dissipated and attending the appointments became somewhat less stressful. At the end of the first trimester, I would venture to say we even entered the ultrasound room with an aura of confidence. The process became routine to us. Reading the data points and measurements on the screen became commonplace. We felt like pros.

Considering our familiarity with the process, we prided ourselves in noting any variant from normalcy. On our next weekly visit, as the technician performed her duties, we noticed the delay in finding the heartbeat. We knew this happened occasionally, and often, Susan could slightly adjust her position, so the heartbeat could be detected. Susan habitually shifted. Nothing. Again, she shifted. Still nothing. This time was different. After many attempts, it was clear that our baby did not have a heartbeat. The technician maintained a sweet demeanor, politely excusing herself from the room to get the doctor's opinion. We knew the reality. The doctor confirmed that we had lost the baby, and with that, we proceeded to the hospital for a D&C[1] procedure.

The doctors sedated Susan, and within a few hours, we were on our way home. Emotionally crippled and our hopes crushed, we entered our home. Without a word, we climbed the stairs to our angelic nursery in hopes of feeling close to our triplets. We asked our babies, our three beautiful guardian angels, for guidance.

---

[1] What is a dilation and curettage (D&C)? A dilation and curettage procedure, also called a D&C, is a surgical procedure in which the cervix (lower, narrow part of the uterus) is dilated (expanded) so that the uterine lining (endometrium) can be scraped with a curette (spoon-shaped instrument) to remove abnormal tissues.

CHAPTER 8

When Change Is the Only Option

Something had to change.

Our support system knew our medical appointment schedule so we anticipated the incoming calls and accepted that we would not be able to lift the burden of heartbreak that we would deliver to those closest to us. They too had found familiarity in their support role and jumped in line as if they had somehow known it would be forthcoming.

My sister, Renae, was the first to be bold enough to suggest a different path that struck a chord with me as a way for me to allow Susan to truly rest while I worked on building our family.

Adoption.

It became clear to me that our specific prayers to get Susan and keep Susan pregnant needed to be altered to "God, please send us the children that we are meant to raise." Our faith didn't waiver with each new turn that our journey took. We talked to Barb about how hard it was to sustain positivity in our efforts to push through the pain while keeping our eyes on our life's purpose; being parents. We remained mindful of the other blessings in our lives, yet we returned to the place that we ultimately felt some sense of connection, the cemetery.

It would have been unfair and insensitive of me to address the topic of adoption with Susan on the evening of the miscarriage. Her head was not in the place of "what do we do next?" She again needed to physically heal in addition to accepting the intense emotions that were presented to her. The disturbing thought that ran rampant in her mind was, "What is wrong with me and why can't I carry a child as easily and naturally as everyone else?"

In addition to the emotions, she was still feeling sickness from the pregnancy hormones, acting as a cruel reminder that she was pregnant, no longer was, and yet had the symptoms that she was more than willing to endure. More on that later.

Although I said it was unfair and insensitive of me to discuss adoption, I didn't say that I didn't do it. We were knocked down and with growing certainty wanted to be parents more than ever, so the only logical step for me was to think of our next move. Almost as if we were in a chess game with life, I continued to play because the love that we had for Nicholas, Mary, and Peter was growing and our angelic nursery remained empty. We were new parents who felt exhausted, but it was from a different type of sleepless nights and the quietness of our home was deafening. "I can work on this next step and give Susan a break," I reasoned to myself.

"Today is as good of day as any to make the call to an adoption agency." And so I did.

I had no intention of making this process more difficult than it had to be. When the agency asked, "Mr. Sirpilla, what type of baby were you looking for?"

My answer came quickly ... "one to love."

I added, "We don't care about gender, ethnicity, or color. We want a baby that needs us as badly as we need him or her."

They responded by saying, "If that's the case, you may find that international adoption may be the best route for you," and I was eager to share the news with Susan.

While being known for my sensitivity, the timing of my insensitivity isn't my proudest moment. It seemed so simple to me. Get our application submitted and get in line to be called. During that time Susan can get on board with adopting. I will work on getting us a baby and she can allow her heart to get to the place that mine was and no time would be wasted.

Susan introduced an obstacle to my plan that I didn't anticipate. While I had experienced our losses from the position of responsibility equally, Susan did not. Meaning, I didn't feel a sense of responsibility greater than she felt and expected that she didn't feel one greater than me. Except that she did. She said to me, "Johnny, I can carry a baby to term, and I would like another opportunity." She continued to explain, "I'm not ready to give up on that dream." She paused and then softly added, "I feel as if I have failed us, our future, and Nicholas, Mary, and Peter."

It was a reminder to me that although we were on this journey together, we were walking on separate paths. We each felt different and unique responsibilities to each other that the other could only partially understand or in some cases, not at all.

For the first time in the past few years, we were not on the same page, and it felt unnatural. The disconnection was not something that we could handle in our fragile state of minds but there was something that I knew for certain. Susan's body was not about to be subjected to more needles, drugs, and surgical procedures. What she felt that she could endure physically was not something that I could endure emotionally for her. This poor girl needed a break ... a break that we could not seem to get but I was determined to find it for her.

I knew my wife's heart. It was as loving and kind as one could be and I inherently knew that if a baby were handed to her, she would embrace the baby and immediately bond as a mother. It was now my turn to do the heavy lifting (with the help of my friend, God) and find that baby.

I completed the adoption paperwork and told Susan, "You don't have to be ready yet because it is a long process. You can pray on it while I take the necessary steps."

What I didn't know was that she was going to need to pray quickly and hear the answer that I wanted her to hear because the adoption agency had twin girls available in Paraguay that were ready to be adopted!

I had shared our history of multiples with the agency and felt as if it was a sign that God had a plan for us and in some way, it was going to be fulfilled. When rational thought and loving support just doesn't fill the void, what do we do? We look for signs to guide us to the right decisions. I'm not going to say that it is the best process to follow in tough times, but I can attest to the fact that if we felt hopeful about a sign, we followed it. Hope was in low supply in our house, and we took it when we got it. We had new hope and that felt fantastic.

A home study was needed to certify state requirements and I pushed, as I'm known to push, to get that completed immediately so we could be on our way to South America in the coming weeks. With my wife's easy-going spirit and openness to God's will, she felt called to accept this opportunity and once again, we were aligned. Alignment and hopeful ... adoption was our path and off to Paraguay we went with suitcases filled with baby girl clothes, diapers and formula. Could it have been this simple all along?

We deserved a break and it looked like one had come our way. Within the next 36 hours, we were going to be holding our newborn twins in a foreign land. As we were racing out the door to the airport, we noticed the answering machine blinking (for the younger reader not familiar with technology of the 1980's and 90's, that is a home device that recorded phone messages on tape when you didn't answer the phone.) Hesitantly, I played the message "Mr. and Mrs. Sirpilla, this is the hospital lab calling to let you know the genetic testing results are in from your recent miscarriage. Your baby was a chromosomally normal female."

We paused in our tracks and looked at each other as the reminder of our pregnancy past caught up with us in a happy moment. We hugged each other, said a quick prayer for her sweet soul, and quickly got in the car. Looking back was not something that we could do. Attempting to process the latest information felt as if it could be too much. We had processed a lot previously and felt comfortable accepting this news as fact and not feeling the need to tie a lot of emotion around it.

This was new to us, right? We were told to let our emotions out, process them to properly deal with them and then move forward in a healthy way. We must have been on process overload, as years of pain had required the processing labs of our brain to work through so much. We were going to take a rain check on this one and just accept it. Easier said than done? Not in this case. Necessity to survive as a couple and fulfill our passion to be parents took over and our girls were in South America waiting to meet their parents. Off we went and nothing was going to stop us.

Or so we thought.

Actually, it was a riot at the airport in Sao Paola, Brazil that was going to cause us to miss our connecting flight to Paraguay. That's what was going to stop us.

+ + +

The international flight attendants could see that we needed assistance and were quick to come to our aide as they got us booked on a flight the next morning and guided us through the riot as Brazilian locals were pounding angrily on the glass dividing walls in the airport, protesting something we didn't understand.

The fear and chaos that we felt clearly left us logically impaired. The airline escorted us to a car that they arranged for us and instructed the driver to take us to a particular hotel. We were instructed to not leave the hotel, or our room and the same driver would be back for us in the morning. The riots were alive in the streets, and we needed to lay low. Through the airline translator, we watched the exchange with the driver and got in the car. Right before being pushed in the car and rushed off to an isolated hotel, the airline personnel grabbed our passports and tickets with a parting message that it was best for them to keep them.

Wait. This is our happy time.

We were in a mode of accepting the facts as they are and avoiding emotional association with each thought. Rioting was violent in the streets as our fate was placed in the hands of an unknown driver. We arrived at a hotel, handed them a note from the airline, and were escorted to our room. Throughout the afternoon and evening in the room, we reaffirmed to each other that our prayer for God to send us the children that we are meant to raise includes this experience along the journey. We had been through much worse, so we accepted it, prayed more and eventually found something to do in the room to pass the time.

It couldn't get worse, could it?

CHAPTER 9

Midnight in Paraguay

The next morning, we remained in prayer that our unknown and unnamed driver would return for us. We held that thought in faith because our intellect had clearly let us down. We were not new to international travel and the magnitude of the misguided action of handing our passports to strangers, in a riot, was not lost on us.

How could we?

Why would we?

What were we thinking?

Those were not questions that we could answer other than realizing that our desperation to become parents had gotten the best of us. We prayed for God's protection in the hours ahead and for a safe arrival in Paraguay to Gabby and Gracie; our twins waiting to meet their parents.

Standing in the hotel lobby in fear that a car would never come, we were more than surprised to see the same man in the same car pull up in front of the hotel. In yet another leap of faith, we piled into the car and headed to the airport. The rioting had calmed down, so we entered the airport and strictly followed the instructions given to us on how to retrieve our passports and tickets. As you can only imagine, at this point, my anxiety was out of control.

Two Americans walking into a Brazilian airport requesting to be handed their passports by strangers without international proof of who we are.

How did we get ourselves in this position?

That was a question for another day, so I clutched Susan's hand firmly and walked with authority as if it was the normal course of international travel. We approached the ticket counter, asked for a supervisor to whom we could explain our story. After a few nerve-wracking translations, we were handed our documents and with the riot under control, walked ourselves to the gate.

Thank You, God.

We were blessed with the opportunity to stay at the home of a friend's cousin and her husband who served as a Christian pastor in Asuncion, Paraguay. It's a city of nearly one million people who were strangers to us but home to our daughters. The family that opened their home to us was kind, faithful and appreciative of our efforts to save two babies from their overcrowded orphanages.

In the routine overview of showing us our room and welcoming us into their home, they were clear and firm on one point. "There has been unrest in Paraguay with Americans adopting their babies," they explained, "therefore you will not be welcomed by many." They continued, "We don't feel it is safe for Susan to be seen on the streets --- she appears 'too American.'" As a full-blooded Italian, I would blend in. So, as long as someone didn't approach me to engage in conversation, my nationality would not serve as a threat.

The adoption agency had arranged for a Paraguayan attorney to pick us up later that evening to take us to the babies. We were told that it would be close to midnight before she picked us up to take us to the orphanage area.

Suspicious, concerned, and alarmed that this was on the up and up? Yes.

Were we willing to alter our plans? No.

So, we watched the clock, as the hours slowly ticked by.

Finally, midnight in Paraguay.

A strong-willed, tall woman came to the door of our host's home. The Pastor wanted to ensure that we were safe and questioned her regarding the time of the meeting and she provided confirmation that it was best for us not to be seen during the day. Another red flag thrown, and we let it fly by. Accepting it for what it was, we got in the car and were driven through the roughest areas of town. Ultimately, we arrived at a small collection of well worn, beat up, old metal shacks the size of a single car garage that served as orphanages to the unwanted babies of the city. We held each other in the back seat of the car, the language barrier preventing us from speaking to the attorney for affirmation. So again, all we could do was pray for God's grace to be upon us.

We cautiously exited the car and walked up to the orphanage. We entered a poorly lit, small room lined with countless rows of cribs with crying babies and genuinely felt that we were exactly where we were supposed to be. Maybe it wasn't in the way that we hoped we would get there but we were about to meet our newborn daughters and one day this would all be part of an adventurous story that brought them into our home.

We walked down the center aisle of the rickety cribs and were taken to the last crib in the room. Expecting to see two newborn babies, we saw one baby who was clearly not a newborn, appearing to be at least four months old. "Where is her sister?" we asked. Through painful attempts at communicating, we were told that the other baby was sick and had to be hospitalized. When questioned about the baby's age, we never received an answer that we could accept or comprehend.

Basically, we were expected to accept that this "newborn" weighed about 20 pounds. She was a beautiful baby, clearly needing loving parents, in an orphanage that lacked the loving environment that all babies deserve. It was heartbreaking to look at the various cribs and wonder what the future would hold for the infants who called this metal shack home. We held her and prayed for God to give us strength to endure this journey for a family and to ultimately bring to us the children that we are meant to raise. If it was this baby, then our hearts were open, but we could see in each other's eyes that something felt "off". It turned out that we would never see that baby girl again.

Prior to travel, we were required to pay for both adoptions in full and at this point were not in the best position to question, but we felt uneasy to say the least. Desperation caused us to take actions that we may not have taken with our minds clear and our emotions in check. It became abundantly clear that we were in a desperate state but there was no turning back now.

The reality that this trip was turning out to be more of a disaster than a blessing was sinking in.

Signs did not appear to be in our favor. So, if we were going to be believers in signs, could we accept the signs that we like and ignore the red flags? It was too early to decide but for the first time, our guard was up.

We returned to the back seat of the attorney's car, holding each other tightly. The crack of gunshots pierced the night as we drove through rough areas of a foreign land that we came to with such hope. Nothing felt right but our history had made clear that our distorted experience of family planning was far off the path of other couples so maybe this was our "normal."

We were dropped off to the welcomed quiet of our host's home around 2:00am and immediately went to our room for some much-needed rest. We prayed for guidance and held each other as we cried in fear about what the next day would bring.

The doorbell rang early in the morning and fortunately our host family was still home to answer to door. It was the Paraguayan attorney standing at the door with a newborn baby boy. This time it was truly a newborn that had not even been bathed since birth hours earlier. The attorney explained to us, "I'm going to the hospital to see the other twin girl and I need someone to watch this baby boy while I'm away." She added, "It would not be safe to bring a newborn into the hospital." Seeing that this baby boy clearly needed to be cared for, bathed, and likely fed, we quickly replied, "We'll watch him!"

To fully appreciate what happens next, I need to insert a quick backstory from my past:

Seven years earlier when I graduated from college, my parents took me to Italy for three weeks of travel and some time spent with our family in my grandparent's hometown. I was able to buy something special as a reminder of my first time in our native country and the special time alone with my parents. I selected a statue of a young man wearing a suit, carrying a briefcase, and hustling through a busy city. I knew that when we returned from our trip, I was going to move to Chicago to start my first job, so I thought the statue would be the perfect gift, rich in symbolism. It was an expensive piece of art that I carried with me, almost like a baby, for the remainder of the trip, as I didn't trust shipping him home.

I decided to give him a name --- Mario Sergio --- and he became the fourth member of our trip.

We joked about where Mario Sergio would like to go for dinner, the sites that he would want to see and the places he knew we should visit, as only the locals would know. Ever since that trip to Italy, many years ago, Mario Sergio, has been prominently displayed in our home so I can remember that amazing time with my parents.

Now, back to Paraguay and that fateful morning.

Before the attorney left, she told us that Paraguay was closing adoptions to Americans the next day. There had been concerns within their country that Americans were adopting babies for impure reasons, which created the tension towards American looking people, like Susan, walking the streets. Before she left, we asked her, "What is this baby boy's name?" that she was leaving with us. As she was turning to leave, she answered over her shoulder.

"His name is Mario Sergio."

The door closed behind her, we turned to each other and smiled.

This is our son.

We gave Mario Sergio a bath, dressed him in pink baby clothes and fed him the American formula that we brought with us. The day went by quickly, pouring our love into a baby that truly needed us. We had saved him from becoming a resident at the horrible orphanage.

Later that evening the attorney returned, and we were told that we could adopt Mario Sergio. She would get the paperwork filed before the deadline and she informed us that she had another baby available for us as well. There was no mention of the baby girl in the hospital and at this point, while we knew that this seemed all too weird, our desperation compelled us to go along with what we were being presented. She returned with a different baby girl that was born a few days earlier and the legal process began.

We named the babies Jake and Gracie and waited for our court date. They slept in our suitcases in our small bedroom, we held them throughout the day and were eager to get up with them during the night.

We had our family.

What could possibly go wrong?

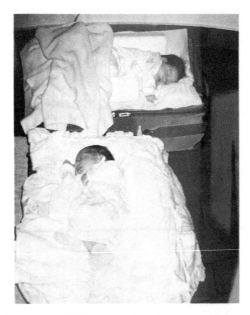

Gracie and Jake sleeping in our suitcases

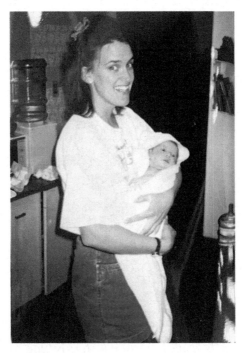

Susan with baby Jake

Johnny with baby Gracie

After returning from Paraguay, we were greeted
with gifts from Johnny's sister, Renae. Stuffed
animals to hold until Jake and Gracie come home

CHAPTER 10

Sadness, Fear and Plenty of Changes

After three weeks in Paraguay and our babies safe with the most wonderful missionary couple to care for them until our return, we headed back to the states to get our careers in order for the coming months.

The adoption would take 4-6 months to finalize, so we found an apartment to rent that would allow us to remain with the babies to bond, love and enjoy the time together in their native land. Susan took a leave from work and would remain in Paraguay full time, and I would go back and forth every few weeks while continuing working.

Was this ideal? Not even a little but it was our life and if our passion for having a family required these lengths, we approached it with a smile and gratitude. Leaving Jake and Gracie felt so unnatural, yet we needed to be practical as young professionals. I can still feel the emotion and tears as we took a taxi to the airport in silence and disbelief that we were leaving the babies that we traveled around the world to meet.

We were met at home with the continued love and support from our family and friends. We immediately got the photographs printed that we took of the babies (long before digital technology) to show our family and friends. Our mothers greeted us with open arms and hope for their new grandchildren. They were meeting them only via pictures since the babies remained in another continent. The nursery was prepared, and our guardian angels were fast at work with two new babies to watch over.

As we temporarily returned to work, we couldn't get the thought out of our minds of Jake and Gracie and the lives we were preparing for them. Life was good, we saw our future, and we held our babies.

At least we thought ...

+ + +

One of the added pressures to the international adoption process was revealed to us while in Paraguay. The country had closed their adoptions to Americans as of September 16th (Susan's birthday). We were assured by the Paraguayan attorney that Jake and Gracie's paperwork was filed on September 14th and 15th so we were not affected since we submitted the documents prior to the closing deadline. A week after returning home, we received a call from our American adoption agency that was facilitating the process to say that there were problems with Gracie's paperwork and her adoption had been denied.

She had to be returned to the orphanage.

A new element of emotion was added to the rollercoaster that we had been living for three years ... anger for the injustice that sweet Gracie would now face. She went from our loving arms and the care of missionaries, truly doing God's work, to the orphanage housed in crude metal shacks with poor nutrition and minimal care. Gracie would return to the painfully dark room of more than a dozen babies in a make shift nursery with no air conditioning. Her life had changed with the stroke of a pen and a "denied" stamp on Gracie Sirpilla's adoption papers. We knew how to deal with sadness and disappointment but injustice and anger for the damage caused to an innocent human life was a different hurdle to navigate. Back to our psychologist, Dr. Barb Fordyce, we went to begin the processing of this loss.

Our natural place to land rested in gratitude. We still had each other. We still had Jake. We still had the most loving support system. Praying for Gracie's future, which we would never know, and while damaged again, we were still together. The hits that kept coming were becoming a norm in this journey for a family, so there was a "belief in the disbelief." While it was hard to get our head around another heartbreak, we held a slight feeling of "I get it ... this is a nightmare, but we will get through it."

Throwing ourselves into our regular routine felt good. We were busy preparing to return to Paraguay while living our normal lives in the states and focusing on the blessing of Jake. In addition to work, I was extremely busy with my volunteer duties at the United Way during allocation season of distributing the funds to the local agencies. It was a beautiful season of focusing on the needs in our community while marveling at the countless community servants who devoted their lives to helping others. Our Wednesday evenings went late ... like until midnight late at times as we were dividing up the funds to the agencies trying to discern one critical community need from the other and assigning dollars to them. It was heavy work but meaningful.

I got in my car around midnight and noticed that I had missed many calls on my "car" phone. My parents were routinely checking in on Susan and found her to be in trouble. Earlier that week she had started her first menstrual cycle after the twin's miscarriage. A normal cycle it wasn't, and she began hemorrhaging that night. She had passed out and fallen in the bathroom and dragged herself through the house leaving a trail of blood. She bruised her ribs in the fall and when my parents got to her, they rushed her to the hospital. They had been there a few hours before I arrived. The stress on my mom and dad's faces told me all that I needed to know. Susan was needing medical care yet again and was back in that all too familiar place ... the hospital bed.

Tests had been run and the doctor came in with results that shocked us. In no possible scenario had we expected to get this news.

Susan's blood tests revealed that she was pregnant.

Based on the blood loss, how could she be pregnant? There was a possibility of pregnancy from our time stranded in Brazil but we never conceived in the traditional way but that could be the only explanation for a new pregnancy. The emotions started to run high with excitement on what this could mean for us, but we tried to not let our minds wonder that far ahead.

An ultrasound soon revealed that the pregnancy hormones registering in the blood test were not a new pregnancy. Susan was still carrying part of the placenta and fetus from the miscarriage two months earlier. We found ourselves in the all too familiar hospital halls where we left a piece of our hearts nearly 9 months earlier when Nicholas, Mary, and Peter were born. How had the time that had passed not improved our position? Was the low that we thought we reached really not "our" low? With Susan's health at risk again, I felt a weakening in me that I can still feel. A buckling at the knees feeling where I truly felt my strength compromised and a need to get to the floor, but I couldn't. Susan deserved better so I needed to find the words to assure her that she is going to be okay, this will all be okay, but the confidence wasn't behind my words and thoughts. Will she really be, okay? Will there be more trauma, pain and sadness coming? And why would we think that it naturally must get better? Maybe it won't and the story doesn't end as we had hoped.

Susan was admitted with the D&C procedure scheduled for the morning. She had the same procedure a few months before so I knew what to expect and how long it would take. We weren't overly alarmed or fearful of the surgery because we understood the frequency in which they are performed and the necessity for Susan. Our kiss goodbye as she was wheeled to the pre-op area was tearful as usual, but we focused on the improved health that she would soon have, and we can continue to move forward with Jake's adoption.

She needed to be healthy to return to Paraguay and we both feared that this setback could impact the adoption.

An hour after the scheduled surgery started my parents, in-laws and I sat in the surgical family waiting area. I was the stereotypical pacer, as I couldn't sit still. We should have had an update saying the surgery was over and she was fine. No news. At 1.5 hours into the surgery, I approached the volunteer desk, asking if they could get me a status update. They obliged while I continued to pace the halls.

As I walked the corridors I saw the OBGYN approaching me, removing her surgical mask but holding a guarded look in his face. I called for my parents and Susan's parents to join me for the surgical update, as I knew that something was off.

My sense was correct. We were stunned by the doctor's first words:

"Susan is alive. It was an extremely difficult surgery."

The weakness in my knees that I felt the previous night was back and I was beyond anxious. The surgery did not go as planned and a major complication had occurred. Susan was alive? What? I had no thought in my mind where she wouldn't still be still living. What had happened that made those words relevant and worth stating?

During the procedure, Susan's uterine wall was perforated, slicing an opening through her uterus. This disastrous turn in the surgery put Susan's life and retaining her uterus at risk. She was excessively bleeding which created complications far beyond what was anticipated. The doctor explained that the massive blood loss made it difficult to see during the procedure. The outpouring of blood required an action to stabilize her, so a balloon filled with water was inserted in her uterus. This would temporarily push off a hysterectomy, stop her loss of blood and save her from bleeding out. A further concern was presented, and it appeared that a placenta site tumor had developed since the last D&C a few months earlier.

I heard the word tumor, and I was done.

Leaning up against the wall couldn't sustain me standing any longer and I slid to the floor in utter disbelief. I was no longer capable to question the doctor. I heard all that I could handle and as my mom tended to me, my dad jumped in with further questions for the doctor. I wanted to do better for our moms and hold their spirits up, but my tank was empty. I had to get myself together prior to Susan getting out of recovery and returning to her room. There was more time ahead for questions and "what next" and I needed to get myself to that point. Susan needed to see me in a better state than I was experiencing currently.

As I waited in Susan's empty hospital room for her to be returned, I felt complete as they wheeled her back in. Something just felt better when we were physically together, and I desperately needed to see her and hold her. Having her feel alone saddened me beyond words. This woman who should be overwhelmed with 9-month-old triplets was alone which wasn't right. This led me to feel that I needed to make it "right" ... what an impossible task, but I desired it, nonetheless. She remained sedated and sleeping, which was okay. I sat at the side of the bed, held her hand, and prayed in thanksgiving that we were together.

The doctor soon followed with more information. There would be more news that I didn't see coming, but I stood as he entered in respect while still holding Susan's hand. He explained that the balloon filled with water that was placed in her uterus to stop the bleeding would be removed in another procedure the following day. The purpose of the balloon was to stop the bleeding to save her life. The alternative was to attempt a hysterectomy, but the excessive bleeding made that too dangerous. The good news was that her uterus was saved, and a hysterectomy wasn't performed. The bad news was that when the balloon is removed, her uterine lining will effectively be "stuck" to the balloon and would come out with the balloon leaving her unable to ever carry a baby with a severely damaged uterus. In addition to the tear, her uterus would seal together, and it would no longer be a healthy organ as it once was.

As the doctor was talking, I became painfully aware that Susan could be coming out of anesthesia at any point and could hear this horrific message. As I turned to look at her, she laid there, still, and silent, with her eyes closed as a gentle tear was streaming from each eye. She heard that she would not be able to carry a child and the discussion about seeing an oncologist to assess the potential tumor. She simply laid there quietly, eyes closed as she reacted privately, without questions or comments soaking in more bad news.

Happiness continued to escape us as the year continued to get worse. We entered the previous New Year with such hope and joy. We should be holding Nicholas, Mary, and Peter with the feeling of being overwhelmed new parents of multiples but instead we are at a point where Susan was fighting for her life in a hospital alone with her thoughts; with our future uncertain.

It was Thanksgiving week, and I was painfully aware that we had so much to be thankful for, yet I was struggling to get there. When I had this feeling over the past months, I would go to the cemetery to be with our kids. Somehow, there was comfort there. They were six feet away from me and I could feel their presence. A sadness was there that was braced in a sense of calm, and I couldn't think of why until this week. Sitting beside Susan's hospital bed, I longed to be at the cemetery, which was unsettling but a place where I just felt that I needed to be. I had the time, so I dove into understanding this drive within me and then it hit me.

At their grave, nothing possibly could be worse, and I was at my bottom. There was nowhere to fall further from there. I felt that our love and our future lay in that grave with a sense of finality that held closure to this nightmare that we were living. That same security escaped me as I watched my resting wife because it wasn't over for us, and we needed to continue, but energy was lost at this point. Hope left us, only to be replaced with fear. She needed to awaken so we could talk, cry together, and plan. I needed to do more for her, but I was powerless as Jake remained in Paraguay held by a government that didn't care about the life he was missing. I chose to find solace in the quiet with Susan at peace. For now, I'd take the quiet as we awaited more medical news. We were referred to an oncologist in Cleveland with tests scheduled in a few weeks to further examine the placenta site tumor.

Over the next several days, Susan recuperated, and she was released the day before Thanksgiving. A holiday with our family at home was just what we needed. Our five nieces and nephews would be there which would bring needed smiles. Their innocence and sweet comments always helped even as they said the things adults wouldn't dare. It was honest and heartfelt which we welcomed.

It was a quiet Thanksgiving weekend until Sunday.

And then it wasn't.

The phone rang and our lives changed.

CHAPTER 11

A Bright Light in a Dark Storm

It was Sunday afternoon after a long holiday weekend.

Dinner at our house with our closest friends, along with my cousin and his wife, was exactly what we needed. We spent the dinnertime with our friend's baby and toddler, as well as my cousin's daughter, all gathered around our kitchen table. With all these wonderful guests, the house was filled with young energy, and we were happy.

We were still processing the week's events with Susan's health and the scary road ahead, which would ultimately delay our return to Paraguay. We needed to ensure that Jake could be watched for a while longer until Susan was healthy enough to return. We would need to contact the missionary couple watching Jake to ask for their patience as Susan healed. Their loving hearts would quickly agree but we didn't want to have more time away from our son.

There was a lot of discussion about the weeks ahead … some fun, some stressful.

And then the phone rang.

Back in the day, we answered the phone without knowing who was calling. I was shocked to hear the voice on the other end of the line --- it was the adoption agency calling on a Sunday. Without trying to draw attention to myself, I casually walked into my office, stepping away from Susan and our guests to have the conversation in private. My heart was racing, and I braced myself for more bad news.

"Johnny, we know that you didn't want an American baby, but a baby was born this weekend, and he is yours if you want him."

I had no words. Silence as my mind was processing this message. I felt as if I was in slow motion and couldn't speak. The agency director filled the silence with some details. "He's a boy, weighing 6 pounds, 3 ounces, delivered 4 weeks early. He's about 10 hours away from you."

"Thank you so much for the call!" I exclaimed as my voice returned. "I need to talk to Susan and then I will call you back."

It wasn't true that we didn't *want* an American baby. We had said that we were open to adopting a baby of any race, any color and from anywhere. The thought of relieving a baby from a life in an orphanage in another country just felt right to us. Couples were waiting years for an American baby, and they were in high demand. Simply, we were drawn to the babies that weren't in high demand and could be forgotten about, so we followed our hearts. There was no desire to *not* have an American baby. We were Americans. We love our country but somehow in our discussions with the agency our preference for an international baby came across as if we didn't want an American baby. We're thankful that they called us despite the misunderstanding. The turn of events in the 10 weeks since we miscarried the second twin was too much to comprehend.

I walked back into the kitchen and Susan was worried. "Is everything okay?" she asked curiously, her brow furrowed.

I replied as calmly as I could, "The phone call was from the adoption agency. They have an American baby. What should we do?"

Susan was in tears and the other two couples immediately questioned me: "So, what did you tell them?"

I calmly replied, "We will call you back."

My calm was met with screaming excitement, almost all in unison. *"Johnny, what were you thinking? Call them back and go get that baby!"*

Within minutes, I called the agency back and said that we wanted the baby boy and would be on the road in the morning to meet him. It was about 8:00 at night so it was too late to start the drive, although the adrenalin that we had pumping could have made the drive easy, a morning departure would be a more responsible decision. We hugged our friends' goodbye, leaving them a messy kitchen in our home and drove over to my parent's house to share the news.

As we walked in their back door, my parents were sitting in their kitchen talking. Before getting our coats off, I loudly blurted out. "Boy, do we have some news for you! The agency just called..." and before I could finish, my dad interrupted, "They are allowing you to adopt Gracie?"

"Nope. An American boy was born the day after Thanksgiving, and we are going to meet him tomorrow."

My parents jumped up, screamed, hugged us, and held on to the feeling of good news coming our way. The natural tendency to want to pull back excitement and wait for it to be finalized was there, but it felt so good to feel this joy. They didn't have the heart to caution us, and we didn't have the desire to challenge it during this moment.

Stepping back a bit – here is some history on our relationship with the adoption agency. It's fair to say that we were "good sports" throughout all that we had endured in the past two months. First, we traveled across the world for newborn twins that weren't newborns. Remember, we never actually saw both babies to confirm if there were in fact twins awaiting our arrival. That was followed by having two babies placed with us, only to have one of them taken away.

Through this process we wanted to be gracious, understanding and accepting that this journey had never been easy and quite frankly shouldn't be easy because we were creating something life changing ... a family. If there were bumps in the road, we would brace ourselves and show the adoption agency that we are in this for the long haul and willing to accept the clear and apparent challenges of adopting a baby. They understood our disappointment, but appreciated our calmness and willingness to get back up and ask, "What can we do next?" They liked us and wanted positive results. We needed them on our side and while it could have been a release to blame them for the missteps, it wasn't going to get us closer to holding our baby. Gracious and understanding ... that's where we needed to stay and so we did.

The agency felt terrible about what happened with Gracie, so when a birth mother randomly called the agency after delivery, they immediately thought of us --- we were their first call. Kindness paid off in a big way and we needed the gesture returned to us for our own survival. We cautioned ourselves that something could go wrong but didn't allow that to weaken our steps towards moving ahead.

Early the following morning, along with my mom, Susan and I started a ten-hour drive to meet our son. Containing the excitement wasn't possible and we didn't even try. Every mile that we drove, we were one mile closer to meeting the boy that was going to change our lives. Eventually, the dark winter drive into the mountains brought a lovely, but early sunset. We were navigating through a part of the country where we had never been, in mountains with snow falling, and pre-GPS navigation, so we were holding tight to a map.

The agency had arranged for us to stay at a house on a lake deep in the mountains which would be too difficult to find on our own, so they told us to meet at a place, interestingly enough called John's Italian Restaurant. How fitting was that? We liked the positive nod that our meeting place was a familiar name, nationality and tied to eating. Pretty fitting for this Italian named John who enjoys good food.

As we pulled into the parking lot, we proceeded to the only car sitting in the lot, and Susan immediately jumped out of the car.

I called out to her, "Wait, Susan, wait!"

Surprised, she turned to look at me as I continued. "We can't meet our son in a dark parking lot. It's too impersonal for this big moment. Tell them that we will follow them to the house."

We had waited this long; another 20 minutes wasn't going to kill us. After all, I needed to have good lighting to film this moment of Susan meeting our son. We pulled into the double car garage of the house alongside the agency ladies.

I reminded Susan, "No peeking … we are in a garage, and this is not going to be the place where we meet our son. Let's get into the house."

The house was nice. It was rustic and modest with a homey vibe that felt comfortable and appropriate for a moment of this magnitude. The car seat, covered with a blanket was placed on the center of the floor in the living room. The unveiling moment had arrived. I scrambled for the camcorder and was ready for Susan to have her moment … our moment. As she removed the blanket, we saw the tiniest little guy that just looked like he was ready to be loved. He was sleeping, peaceful and perfect.

Susan unbuckled him from the car seat, pulled him out and while smiling from ear to ear said, "I'm your mom. It's so nice to meet you."

The emotion was flowing, and the moment was incredible. Life changing in every way. Here in these dark mountains, on a quiet lake, ten hours from home, alongside my mother, we met our son. We decided on his name during the long drive. The triplet boy names were planned to be Johnny, Jake, and Beau. When we had Nicholas, Mary, and Peter we decided to save the original names for future children and honor our family members by naming the triplets after them. We chose John Anthony (my full name) for our son in Paraguay and since I already was called "Johnny", we chose to call him Jake. So, with two of our names taken, we were now looking at our son, Beau. Beau Harris Sirpilla. Harris was Susan's mom's maiden name and our mutual love and adoration for her made the decision easy to have a part of her legacy with our newborn son.

After a few hours holding Beau and just resting in the love and gratitude that we felt, the agency shocked us with another surprise.

The birth mother wanted to meet us.

She was waiting for us at their office.

Susan responded with a quick, "Yes, of course. Let's go."

I, however, didn't land there. I was holding my son. I wasn't leaving my son. And the strangest thoughts came to my mind. Usually, I'm a people person. I love to dig in, seek to understand others, and explore who they are and what drove them to certain decisions. It would appear that this would be an ideal setting for that exploration. It could be a once in a lifetime meeting with endless questions.

Yet, I was feeling no interest in getting off the couch with my son.

Wow, this was weird. Feelings that were new and unfamiliar. I was truly not interested. How could I be so rude and ungrateful? While having an appreciation for the feelings that I felt, I was content, which was unlike me. I was always inquiring and wanting to engage. But now, I wasn't moving. I had my son and the only place I could ever imagine being was with him.

Susan noticed that I wasn't getting up and as she turned to embark on this meeting together, I shook my head and explained, "I'm good. Beau needs me here and this is where I need to be."

Fortunately, my mom was with us, and she spoke up. "I'd love to go and meet her." Perfect. Susan wouldn't be alone in this rare meeting and my mom would now be in a chapter of Beau's life that was better fitted for her than me. What's especially significant about my mom's willingness to volunteer is that initially she wasn't fully subscribed to the idea of adopting a baby. It wasn't that she didn't love children and especially her own and her other grandchildren, but she had a reservation that she couldn't quite verbalize. Maybe the magnitude of the topic was too much to get her head around, so she was guarded. Guarded until she met Beau and then her world changed. Her love was immediate and no less intense than what she felt for Nicholas, Mary, and Peter or her other 5 young grandchildren. Her life and views had been changed with one look at her grandson. There was something so beautiful in the openness she felt to expanding her heart so naturally and effortlessly.

The meeting with his birthmother was filled with emotion and honesty. The women, two strangers' moments before, shared a deep life interaction that would be short lived but long lasting. Susan thanked her for making the choice of adoption as opposed to abortion and trusting us with this incredible gift. His birthmother asked Susan to give him the life that she could not and as they both cried, they hugged and said goodbye.

We had our son, and it was time to return to Ohio and face the upcoming medical appointments for Susan. We had a placenta site tumor to deal with and a reality to face that could make this joy we were feeling short lived.

Meeting Beau

Johnny holding Beau for the first time

CHAPTER 12

Reframing Our Thoughts

The first night with Beau was truly magical. I repeated the same statement to him on that first night followed by countless other nights …

"So, you're the little guy that we've been waiting for. It's so nice to meet you."

The term "so nice to meet you" had never had such significance. Said without thought many times, it really had meaning to us that was life changing. Meeting Beau really did change our lives. When we held Nicholas, Mary, and Peter, it felt natural. They were ours. Holding Beau felt *exactly* the same. How could that be?

Society's words around adoption confused me and really didn't prepare me for what I was feeling. People would say things like:

"If you can't have one of your own, adoption is the next best thing."

"Do you know anything about his 'natural' parents?"

The early days of confusion quickly wore off. We processed what we had heard but couldn't relate those words with the way that we felt. Quite simply, Beau *was our own* and there was nothing *unnatural* about us as his parents. The comments were all well intended but simply lacking exposure to adoptions. Society had their own thoughts around adoption, which was fine, but they simply didn't apply to our family.

God created Beau to be our son --- Beau Sirpilla. We accepted that from the beginning and would proudly raise Beau to feel the same. We weren't naïve enough to think that he wouldn't need time as he matures to process the concept. To be fair, we processed the idea of adoption with the maturity of our 29-year-old minds. He deserved the right to process it as a 3 year old, 5, 10, 15, 20 and well into adulthood. What we knew was simple. Our love was rooted in gratitude for the gift of getting to be Beau Sirpilla's parents and we would simply live in that gratitude.

We learned to have fun with introducing adoption to those who had not experienced it before. Never offended, we knew their hearts. We still joke today about one of my best's friends who asked, "How tall is Beau's dad?"

My reply came quickly, *"I'm 6'1", why do you ask?"*

+ + +

Back to the early days. There was a 10-day period when the birth mother could change her mind and we needed to ensure that the birth father signed off on his rights to parent. I'm not going to lie -- those 10 days were tough. Beau quickly became the center of our world and that simply couldn't change. With confirmation on the 10th day that they had both signed over legal rights, we were relieved, but next we had to pass several home visits from the Child Services Agency and then appear in court 6 months later for the formal adoption.

Life was as good as we could have imagined, but there were a few nagging thoughts lurking in our minds. Most pressing was the upcoming testing and doctor's appointment at the Cleveland Clinic to address Susan's placenta site tumor. As a mother now with the responsibility of a newborn, she was no longer only accountable to herself --- Beau needed a healthy mother. We knew we had to prepare ourselves for tough news ahead and follow the doctor's recommendations to address her tumor. We had the films and medical notes from radiology ready for our appointment that was just a few weeks away. Our plan was to be joyful as possible because Beau deserved our fullest attention. We could push the medical issues a few weeks down the road. Those thoughts can wait. They had taken enough of our attention for the past three years.

There was another topic I struggled with more than Susan … not surprising based on our personalities and my tendency to worry. I was so incredibly happy with Beau and watching Susan with him. It's hard to genuinely express the joy we felt with evening baths, bottle feedings, diaper changes, getting up in the middle of the night to feed him … all of it. It was simply the best. But with this new reality, I was carrying the other existing reality that our first three babies were in a grave. Could I have moved on that easily and forgotten them? This became a frequent topic of conversation in our counseling sessions with Barb.

In one particular session with Barb, I confessed what I was thinking: "I simply will not let go of Nicholas, Mary, and Peter."

"Why not? Barb gently probed.

"It feels wrong, disloyal, and not what a good father would do." I paused, continuing to gather my thoughts. "Holding on to them means staying in sadness that they had died in our arms. I am willing to stay there if that means I stay connected to our first three children."

"I see," Barb answered.

"I feel these feelings deeply within me," I added. "I have to keep that connection to them."

It was at that point that Barb introduced a concept that changed my life. She worked diligently with us for several years, as we learned to *reframe our thoughts* to ones that we could accept and live with. Erasing our thoughts wasn't possible, there were far too many, but reframing them in a light that we could accept and carry forward was a mindset that had to be achieved to move ahead. And with this, Barb said the following in reply to my statement that I refused to let go of them. As I said, her wisdom changed my life.

"Johnny, you don't have to let go of Nicholas, Mary, and Peter, but you do have to let go of the dreams that you had for them in this life because they will not be."

Life changing. She made it clear. I don't have to let go of them. I can hold on to them as tightly as I desire and have the permission now from a trusted professional that my deep-rooted need to hold on to them was healthy and acceptable. However, I did need to let go of the dreams for raising them, teaching them sports, going to their school performances, and watching triplets become best friends as they grew up together. Their graduation, weddings and all of life's milestones would not be. But I could still be their dad, hold on to them while letting go of those dreams.

Reframing thoughts. I now had a plan that I could work towards. I had their funeral professionally videotaped because it was the only sacrament in the church that we would have with them. I didn't know if I would ever watch it, but I wanted the option to go back to the day of celebrating their life while saying goodbye. I wanted their brothers and sisters-- hopefully that followed-- to have the opportunity to experience a part of their older sibling's lives however sad it may be. I have watched the funeral many times and still find beauty and comfort.

+ + +

Back to Susan's health. Beau was about 4 weeks old, and it was time for Susan's appointment. Parenting him sustained us through the anxiety leading up the appointment and we entered the vast medical facility that is the Cleveland Clinic. Going for testing followed by a meeting with an oncologist was going to set the course for our lives ahead. Had the tumor grown? What is the risk for malignancy? When is surgery to remove it? The questions busied our minds, and the tension grew.

We were supported by our village of friends and family who prayed for Susan's health, along with endless calls of love and encouragement leading up to the appointment. As we sat in the exam room waiting for the doctor to arrive with the results, we felt as if her fate was looming, and a final verdict was going to be rendered. It was overwhelming. We were finally happy. It could not change now.

The doctor entered. "I've compared your films from last month to your films today and I'm puzzled. The mass was evident last month, but on today's films, there is no mass."

No mass?

No words. We sat there in shock. It never entered our minds that this could be the outcome of the appointment. No further action needed. She's okay. Go home and live. And we did just that.

My immediate response?

I wanted to get out of there as quickly as possible before the news changed.

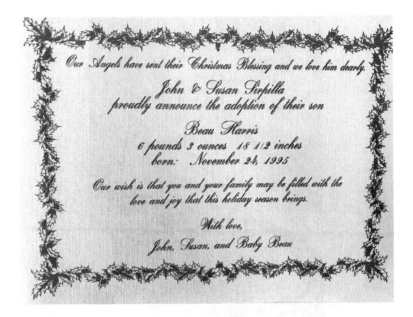

Our Angels have sent their Christmas Blessing and we love him dearly.

John & Susan Sirpilla
proudly announce the adoption of their son

Beau Harris
6 pounds 3 ounces   18 1/2 inches
born: November 24, 1995

Our wish is that you and your family may be filled with the
love and joy that this holiday season brings.

With love,
John, Susan, and Baby Beau

Beau's birth announcement photo

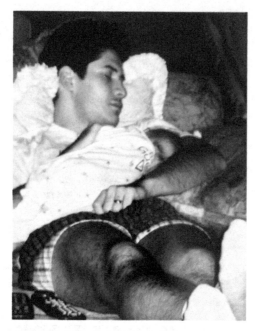

Nap time with Beau

Beau's first professional photos with his three angels

CHAPTER 13

Angels Among Us

The months flew by, and we were enjoying every moment of being Beau's parents.

The boy rarely napped other than in our arms. We knew it wasn't the best for his eventual sleep habits, but we simply couldn't put him down. Holding him and dreaming for his future brought feelings that filled our hearts beyond what we could have dreamed. As my mind would have it, I kept thinking about Nicholas, Mary, and Peter. Every time we entered Beau's nursery; they were present. The angels in the sky hanging over his crib brought comfort and yet a reminder that they weren't here.

It was often that I sought out their approval that my happiness was okay with them. I asked for signs that they were happy, together, and watching us. One day when Beau was about 10 months old, I was home alone with him on a Saturday afternoon as Susan was out running errands. It was naptime, and I took advantage of the opportunity, yet again to be part of his nap by holding him and enjoying the closeness and innocence as he slept on me. The song by the band Alabama, "Angels Among Us" was a frequent song played in our home as it brought us a lot of comfort.

It was getting late and I was scared and alone
Then a kind old man took my hand and led me home
Momma couldn't see him oh but he was standing there
And I knew in my heart that he was the answer to my prayer

Oh, I believe there are Angels Among Us
Sent down to us from somewhere up above
They come to you and me in our darkest hours

To show us how to live
To teach us how to give
To guide us with a light of love

When life held troubled times
And had me down on my knees
There's always been someone
To come along and comfort me

A kind word from a stranger
To lend a helping hand
A phone call from a friend just to say I understand

And ain't it kind of funny
At the dark end of the road

Someone lights the way with just a single ray of hope

The song was blaring loudly, and Beau was fast asleep with his head resting on my shoulder and his little chubby arms wrapped around my back. I walked around the house with the song on repeat and just savored the moment with Beau. It was making a deep imprint on my mind. I was praying for his future, his safety, and thanking God for the blessing of being his dad.

And then I said the following: "Nicholas, Mary, and Peter, would you forgive me for being so happy and in love with your little brother? I promise that my love for you is not diminished by my love for Beau. If I could have all four of you in our home, it would be more than we ever wanted!"

Following that confession, I finished with a request. "Would you show me a sign that you are in peace, happy and still with us?"

And then chills went down my spine.

As Beau was in the deepest sleep as I held him, with his head resting on my right shoulder, I noticed movement of his sweet little hand on my left shoulder. As he was drooling and sleeping soundly, his chubby hand patted the back of my shoulder *three* times. The sign I had asked for was granted and while Alabama was singing about Angels Among Us, I was living it. Their spirit was with us, and I felt they were connected to Beau in a way that I needed them to be, and they were right where they were supposed to be. Not in our home physically but in our hearts permanently.

+ + +

Beau was born almost exactly 9 months to the day that the triplets had died. It felt as though as they had left this earth, Beau was conceived and destined for us. They were at peace and now I was too.

Beau's first birthday was an emotional celebration. I couldn't miss the opportunity to publicly thank our closest friends, my sisters, and parents for staying so close to us during the journey that led to this day of celebration. We were still fighting with the Paraguayan government to get Jake home. It had been over a year with delays and the missionary couple was kind enough to send us photos of our growing son. We spoke to Beau a lot about his brother Jake that he would soon be meeting, but we were growing weary and now realizing how attached Beau was to us, we feared how hard it would be for Jake to leave who he knew to be his parents.

As Jake turned 14 months, we made a decision that would change his life and ours. He needed to be with his permanent family and no longer in waiting for us. The mission that this amazing missionary couple served limited them to one adoption and they had already adopted twins after raising their full-grown children. Since they were not an option to parent Jake, we asked them if they could find a Paraguayan couple to adopt him. We soon heard from them that a doctor and his wife would be adopting John Anthony Sirpilla II, "Jake".

We had now come to realize that coincidences don't exist, and we are connected in ways that we couldn't imagine. The doctor we took Jake to when we were there and who had taken care of him for the first 14 months of his life went to a family celebration for his brother and his wife to meet the new baby they adopted. When the doctor arrived, he said,

"You adopted Jake Sirpilla. He is my patient."

In a city with one million people, Jake's doctor was now his uncle. Our hearts were full, and we accepted that we had served the role in Jake's life that we were meant to serve. As of this writing, we are told that Jake is in medical school to become a neurologist. Our role in Jake's life was to save him from that orphanage and we did just that. His life was forever changed because Nicholas, Mary, and Peter Sirpilla existed. Their lives had significance spanning the globe. Jake may never know the role they played in his life, but we do, and it makes our journey to Paraguay worth every intense moment.

+ + +

Shortly after Beau's first birthday we received a call from the adoption agency. Concerned, we gladly took the call. Beau's birth mother was pregnant again and they wanted to know if we would support her during her pregnancy and adopt the new baby. We couldn't have said yes fast enough. We knew that we could provide for Beau so many wonderful things in life, but a biological sibling was something that we never imagined for him.

The support process began, and we received regular updates about doctors' appointments and how she was doing with her pregnancy. Our hearts were so full that Beau would have a sibling, so the planning began.

We had a break for a year regarding Susan's health but there was an issue that we felt needed to be addressed medically. During the D&C after the miscarriage of the second twin, Susan's uterus was perforated with the surgical knife. While it wasn't presenting a problem, we felt that if something could be done so her uterus could be healthy, we should take those steps. We had no plans to attempt pregnancy again as our family was blessed with adoption and that was our path, but we thought it was prudent to see a specialist.

We were referred to an Egyptian doctor who was kind beyond belief and felt that a surgical procedure was necessary to repair the tear so her uterine wall would be strengthened while addressing Asherman's Syndrome[2] which was a result of the last surgery. As per usual, Susan agreed to the surgery and felt no pressure with a growing son and another on the way. She underwent the surgery at a Cleveland hospital, and

---

[2] Asherman's syndrome is **an acquired condition where scar tissue (adhesions) form inside your uterus**. The scar tissue can build up, decreasing the amount of open space inside your uterus. This condition can be a complication of medical procedures or cancer treatments.

we returned to the doctor's office 6 weeks later for testing and to hear the level of success he achieved.

His words were discouraging. "Susan, your uterus is no longer a healthy organ. After your miscarriage, the D&C procedure left your uterus fused together. I was able to stitch up the area that was torn but not able to remove the Asherman's Syndrome that has developed." Continuing, he said, "You should not pursue IVF because it will never yield a pregnancy and in fact, you could never carry a baby safely to term. Your life, as well as the baby's, will be at risk. There is not enough room for a baby to grow and would likely be deformed. The placenta could be pushed into your other organs and create other life-threatening complications."

This was a lot to digest. We told him that we were practicing Catholics and did not use birth control. Should we consider this intervention now to protect Susan?

His answer was astonishing. "I respect your religious views, so you leave that up to God."

We left his office with heavy hearts but so thankful for Beau and his new sibling that was due in September. It was springtime so we would enjoy our summer with Beau and prepare to become parents again.

Or so we thought ...

Nap time with Beau

Beau's adoption court hearing

All smiles with Beau

CHAPTER 14

Another Baby?

The months flew by as we soaked up loving Beau.

We were receiving periodic updates from the adoption agency reminding us that we are in fact expectant parents. We gladly supported his birth mother through this new pregnancy because the gift of a biological sibling for Beau would assist him in the future if he ever felt "alone" or "different". In fact, he and this baby would have the only biological connection in our family. Susan and I don't share that connection, we don't share it with Beau, but he would have this connection that we're told is so important. It didn't mean anything to us because the issue of biology meant nothing in our minds because we had our son ... we were set! But if this could ease any concerns for him and we get another child in the process, it was a win-win!

The long-awaited call came, and a baby boy was born. We loaded up the car with our new infant gear, invited our mothers to experience the gift of welcoming our new son into the family and the 10-hour drive began. It was even better than last time because we had our 18-month-old son to hold on to as we took this journey. Telling him about his new baby brother made the trip so enjoyable and with deep meaning.

We checked into our hotel, got some rest, and awoke to the day that we would meet our new son. The pick-up point was set so we just needed a time to be there. We sat by the phone waiting for further instruction. Patience is not yet a virtue that I have developed so the waiting became painful as an hour passed, then two, and finally we got the call. "The birth father's parents are not supportive of her decision to place the baby for adoption. They are talking and will get back to us when they have decided."

Wait ... how is this happening?

We knew that it was a different birth father, but we had never heard any concern throughout the pregnancy that this was an issue. We supported her as agreed with the knowledge that she had done this before and was comfortable with her last decision, which is why she chose to do it again. Fear of losing this opportunity for our family filled all our minds as we sat in the hotel stunned.

We woke up the following morning to the news that Princess Diana was killed in a car accident. The four of us were glued to the TV as the world had just changed. This beacon of light, the people's princess was gone, and it became one of those tragedies that we knew would be marked in our minds forever in terms of where we were and what we were doing. While fixated on the TV, we waited for the phone to ring. And waited ... to finally hear that she will continue to go through with the adoption, and we can pick our son up late in the afternoon. We just needed to get through the day and focused on the TV to try to gain some understanding and belief that Princess Diana was gone.

"Later that day" turned into rescheduling the pickup for the following morning and it began to sink in that we had a problem. Two days later with empty promises and broken hearts the five of us packed up the car and headed home. We told the agency that we will come back at any time if she changes her mind, realizing that parenting isn't ultimately what she wants to do.

We arrived back in Canton around midnight feeling thankful for having Beau to hold on to and pour our love into. We laid him in his crib with the angels looking over him and we felt some peace in knowing that our guardians will continue to be with us. Turning to them for strength was natural as we felt them so close to us. We needed them. Just being in their bedroom brought comfort.

The following morning was Labor Day. We had plans to be at my sister Laura's house for a family day, which was clearly needed. Beau would be with the people who made him the happiest, his cousins, and we could have some time to process and talk through this latest disappointment.

Susan was showering as I was feeding Beau and getting him dressed. I walked into the bathroom and noticed a change in Susan's body that was the first physical change in her past pregnancies. I'll be a gentleman again and refrain from sharing the details, but I knew that she looked different than she did the last time I looked. ☺ I asked when she had her last period and she shrugged it off with "I don't know."

"Come on, Susan, think. I need to know .... Heck, you need to know."

Susan thought for another moment, then replied, "It's been a few months."

"A few months? Do you think you're pregnant? We need to take a pregnancy test!"

"I'm not pregnant," she scoffed, "and I'm not taking a test. You know it will be negative."

You all know me well enough by now. I was not letting this go. We got Beau buckled in his car seat and headed to the drug store before going to my sister's. I insisted on a pregnancy test before the Labor Day celebration, and she obliged me as if I were a pesky younger brother annoying her.

We drove back home from the drug store, and she went in to take the test. Beau and I waited in the car and within a minute she came outside and yelled, "The test is positive. What do we do?"

We laughed until we couldn't laugh anymore. We jumped up and down until I realized that Susan shouldn't be jumping. We cried until we realized that we were scaring Beau. Way too many emotions swirling.

The doctor told us in April that the surgery wasn't a success, and she could never conceive.

He told us a pregnancy would put Susan's life and the baby's life at risk due to severe likely complications. But he also said that she would never get pregnant because her uterus was filled with scar tissue. So how did this happen?

There isn't room for a baby to grow due to the large amount of scar tissue.

But right now, we're pregnant! And that felt amazing. Can we feel this good with so much to worry about? For now, the answer was "heck yeah!" and we felt great.

Within minutes, we were at my sister's house and greeted by the entire family. They approached us with sad eyes, the need to hug us so we could feel their support and a desire to make this a happy family day so we could take a break from thinking about the disappointment that crushed us yesterday. A failed adoption has a mourning process much like any other loss, so their hearts were in the right place.

After the Italian welcoming from so many with hugs that we needed, the smiles on our faces were hard to conceal. I announced, "We have a baby update."

Almost to a person, they called out, "She changed her mind and you're going back to get the baby?"

"No" I said. "……….. Susan's pregnant."

The room went quiet. No words. Well, only two words from my dad.

"Oh, sh$%!"

It was his honest reaction, and we couldn't fault him. Do we celebrate? Do we panic as a group? There was no protocol on which we could lean for direction. Our family knew the risks associated with another pregnancy, so it was a lot of information to process in a short time.

In reflection as I write this, it was almost cruel to put them through yet another rollercoaster ride that would land on uncertainty. Yet, this was our reality. The overload of questions hit us, and we had little answers. I knew that I had to get back in my "pregnant Dad" mode and I had work to do. We needed an ultrasound ... TODAY.

I called our high-risk pregnancy doctor, Dr. Prab Gill and pleaded for a favor. We needed to see how far along Susan was and if we had a viable pregnancy. The kindness in this man, I can't explain, and he agreed to meet us at the hospital for testing.

The ultrasound revealed a strong heartbeat and the baby measured between 10-11 weeks. Susan was almost three months pregnant!

We were pregnant but not sure how to feel or where to go for medical care. We loved Dr. Gill but walking into the hospital brought so many emotions back from the past two years. We felt as though we needed a fresh start. We had no doubt in the quality medical care we would receive but emotionally we were on fumes and had to change something. Although it wasn't convenient, we selected a high-risk doctor in Cleveland and committed to making the weekly drive for ultrasounds and checkups. He confirmed the high-risk pregnancy situation, reviewed the surgery films from earlier in the year to understand the location of the tear in Susan's uterus, her Asherman's Syndrome, and would monitor the pregnancy closely.

Within a week, Susan began spotting and the signs of miscarriage were glooming. The frantic call to the doctor's office yielded little relief as we were told to rest and wait and see over the next few days. If there were no more bleeding, we would see them on Friday's scheduled ultrasound. Resting wasn't easy with an 18-month-old, along with the fear that we both had, but we had been in this position before so we could handle it. The spotting lessened and on Friday we had a strong heartbeat. The baby that was continuing to grow!

By 16 weeks gestation, we felt confident that the miscarriage time was behind us and the concern of Susan's uterus stretching as the baby grew became our new focus. Our next weekly appointment revealed a new concern that we didn't anticipate. Susan was 75% effaced which meant the cervix was shortening, becoming softer and thinner in preparation for birth. This threw off new alarm bells and Susan was placed on complete bed rest. She was allowed bathroom privileges and showers every other day. Otherwise, she was completely on her back with our bed in the Trendelenburg position, which meant the foot of the bed was put up on cinder blocks to take pressure off her cervix. She would be lying inverted until the baby was born ... in 5 ½ months!

We adjusted our routine accordingly and accepted life in our bedroom around the clock. We had the most wonderful nanny who loved Beau dearly and was at our house to cover my work hours, so she could get Susan food, bring toys to her bed for Beau, and ensure they were both safe until I got home each evening. The fresh smell of play dough in our bed, along with finding random toys waiting to surprise me as I laid down with Susan became a daily routine, but it made me happy.

We lived Friday to Friday. It was the big day that I would help Susan get dressed, walk her downstairs, and get in the car for the hour drive to the doctor's office for our checkup and ultrasound. We reminded them weekly to not reveal the sex of the baby, as we believed there are few joyful surprises in life as great as hearing the announcement of your son or daughter in the delivery room. Life was quiet and good. Our faith group meetings were held in our bedroom every other Wednesday night, so our house was filled with love and people that cared about us.

As we approached 26 weeks into the pregnancy, we were believing that this miracle baby really could become a reality. In my quest for staying busy on a Sunday afternoon, Susan gave me a project and decided that it would be fun to switch our living room and dining room furniture … just for a change. We were spending a lot of time in the house, and we needed a change of scenery. On a bathroom break, Susan was interested to see my progress and design talents, so she came to the balcony area and looked down at my efforts. She was near the top of the steps and with infrequent movement was a little shaky to say the least.

Before I knew it, she lost her balance and fell down the stairs.

I raced to meet her before she reached the bottom to break her fall. This couldn't have happened. The baby! God, please let the baby be okay.

I got Susan back in bed, she hysterical and me seeking medical advice. We couldn't feel movement with the baby immediately and surely, he or she couldn't be sleeping after the fall, but the doctor's office said to remain calm, watch for bleeding and signs of labor. We did just that and as the hours passed, she said the baby was moving and for now, no labor.

It was just another scare and another typical day in the life of Johnny and Susan's journey for a family.

Susan remained in bed for the next few months and our routine of living in one room of our house became a way of life. We were happy, content, and preparing Beau to become a big brother.

At nearly 35 weeks, Susan went into labor, and it was progressing quickly. It came on fast and hard. With the hour drive to our doctor, we didn't feel that we had the time to make it, so I called Dr. Gill and he said that we needed to get to Aultman Hospital where Nicholas, Mary, and Peter were born. We trusted him and felt that was the best place to be examined. The baby wasn't due for 5 more weeks so we thought it could be false labor and we would be sent home.

Upon examination he confirmed that due to the previous tear in her uterus, she could not go into further active labor with frequent contractions. An emergency C-section was needed, and he would take good care of us. Susan wanted to leave the hospital … very real PTSD was racing through her mind and lovingly he told her. "This baby will live and be okay, but if you leave this hospital, I can't promise that same outcome."

The decision was simple. It's time to have a baby.

As the surgical team was being assembled and preparing the operating room, Dr. Gill talked to us about the importance of tying Susan's tubes during the surgery to prevent another pregnancy. Her uterus had been through too much trauma, and this needed to be her last pregnancy. We looked at each other with our eyes meeting and we knew the answer without saying it. We trusted in God to get us to this delivery, and we are holding to that trust and not removing the opportunity for Him to perform another miracle in our lives. Our hearts would remain open, and we would trust in His protection over us.

We couldn't consent to tying her tubes.

Into the operating room we went.

CHAPTER 15

"Is Her Real?"

All we could do was laugh.

As Susan and I waited in her hospital room to be taken into the operating room, we couldn't help but laugh. The hospital waiting room was filled with family and friends and we were about to experience something really joyful. Fear was nowhere to be found, but we seemed to laugh a lot. Laughed at the happy reality of what was happening within the next hour. We could not comprehend our reality without laughter.

I told Susan that I thought before making the incision that they should do one more pregnancy test to make extra sure that we are in fact pregnant. We laughed again realizing the disbelief we had in the reality that we were actually experiencing. No legal documents to sign, no court process to make the baby legally ours, no one that could take the baby from us. This is what other couples experience all over the world in a very normal course of action and through pain, endurance and trust it was now our turn. It felt great to laugh and feel grateful.

Susan was calm on the all too familiar operating table and as they put up a screen so she couldn't see the work being performed on her, I shifted from standing behind the curtain near her head to glancing over to see what was happening. As the doctors were performing the C-section, we tried to guess the sex of the baby, but of course, neither of us had a clue. We wanted a girl because we had a boy but again, we still couldn't grasp the reality that we were having a baby that we could take home. The gender question would be answered soon enough, and we couldn't wait.

It was time! Cutting into her abdomen was complete and the doctor was reaching in to pull out the baby. I'll never forget his words as he said, "It's a ...(and now the head was out)... It's a ... (as the shoulders came out) ... It's a ..... GIRL!"

Laughter and tears combined. The baby was 5 weeks premature but actively crying and appearing very healthy. Isabella Grace was in our arms but understanding of the magnitude of what we just experienced was lost on us. We were floating somewhere, and my mind had a lot to process. While holding Bella and showing her to Susan as they continued the surgery to close her up, a strong feeling came over me. As I stared into her tiny eyes, a familiarity hit me.

I saw her sister, Mary.

They shared the same features and the thought that I was holding a portion of my first daughter as I held this new daughter was something that could not escape me. I wasn't looking for a comparison. It was simply just there.

As an aside, before Mary passed away, she took her little hand and tucked it under her chin bending her wrist with her hand facing down. To this day, Bella sleeps the same way with her hand nestled under her chin, bent wrist facing down. She slept like that as a baby, as a little girl and still does as an adult. I think of her big sister every time I see her in that position. What an amazing feeling of connectedness and having Mary with us.

Back to the day in the hospital …

Keeping the sex of the baby a surprise provided one of the most joyful moments in my life. I now had the honor of going out to a waiting room filled with the people that we loved most and announce, "It's a girl!" to the support system who had been with us every step of the way.

This wasn't just our moment, it belonged to our village that carried us on the days that we couldn't think of walking, loved us when our thoughts were so dark that we couldn't feel love, and encouraged us to be faithful to our focus to build a family without consideration for leaving each other or our dreams. I don't know if I have ever delivered news that brought people to a level of relief, bliss, and love as I did in this experience. It was magical.

Assuring them that Susan was doing great, and "Bella" would soon be on her way to the regular nursery and not the pediatric intensive care unit as we had thought due to her prematurity was like oxygen to them. They all *needed* that news and could exhale.

Later in the afternoon, my parents went to our house to get Beau to meet his new baby sister. To him, becoming a big brother was a big deal and at just 2 years old, he fully comprehended that this baby grew in Mommy's belly, and he grew in Mommy's heart. This dialogue helped Beau understand his adoption from the very beginning because as he was learning to speak, he was also asking intuitive questions such as "Was I in Mommy's belly?"

Thinking quick on our feet became a common theme, as Beau was wise beyond his years. So, we adapted to his questions and became ready for the next. As I carried Beau into the hospital room, he needed to hug his mom before he could think of meeting his sister. As if he was alarmed seeing her in a hospital bed, he needed that hug of reassurance that his mom was okay. I carried him over to the basinet and he looked over his sleeping sister.

"Is her real?" he quietly uttered with his hoarse voice.

What a question! I think he was as disbelieving as we were that a baby was actually coming.

It felt great to reassure him, "Yes, bud … her is real."

"I want to kiss her."

"You do that, Beau. Bella will always need her big brother, so let her know you're here."

And he has been there for her ever since. And she for him.

+ + +

Back to the "processing" that I mentioned in the delivery room. The day moved along smoothly with a lot of love and gratitude but … I know there shouldn't be a "but" in this setting, yet my active thinking mind was having some processing issues. I found myself getting a little quiet and withdrawn but the time to figure out what was distracting me from unbelievable happiness wasn't now.

As it became nighttime, I needed to take Beau home to get him to bed and Susan needed some quiet time to rest. I got Beau to sleep and my mother-in-law, a woman who held all the qualities that I loved about Susan, was staying at our house. She could deliver honesty in a loving way, and we were close enough for her to say what she was about to say. "Johnny, you weren't yourself today and I'm concerned to know what's going on."

Bummer … an actor, I am not. What I was feeling was apparent to others, which was not my intent. I said, "Mom, today was just a lot and I need some time to process it all." But I wasn't sure what it was that I needed to process.

I woke up in the middle of the night, went downstairs for the all too familiar bowl of cereal to suppress the insomnia. Sitting at the table in a dark kitchen, I needed the quiet of the night to wrestle with the uneasy feeling that I had that was perplexing. It was something that I didn't want to carry into the new day at the hospital.

I reviewed the events of the last 24 hours in my mind and wrestled to think what could possibly cause mental unrest as opposed to me feeling a new stratosphere level of happiness.

And then it hit me. A thought came into my head, but I didn't like the words attached to it.

"She seems nice, but she's not Beau."

What in the world does that mean? And why am I thinking it?

It took a little more time for me to realize the comparison that I was making based on the societal norms that I grew up hearing and having them reinforced throughout the pregnancy from innocent comments.

By comparison to having Beau handed to us, having Bella handed to us felt the same. Yet, some people said, "We're so excited that you're going to have one of your own." Does that imply that this was supposed to feel stronger, greater, or superior to having a baby that we didn't have a biological connection to? At some level, I think that I must have also believed that having a biological child was going to be a supreme level of joy that we had yet to experience. But to me, knowing the depth of love that I had for my 2-year-old, I didn't have stronger feelings for her. I didn't really know her yet and I'm supposed to feel more for her than an adopted child? I didn't feel it, so it meant one of two things. I'm deficient, as a biological father because the connection in our biology should elicit feelings that I wasn't feeling. Or the issue of biology wasn't the lead story and defining trait of what defined my love for my two children.

I quickly landed on the latter and affirmed to myself that Susan and I will create our own norms for our family and what society dictated in clichés or uninformed comments wouldn't survive in our household. I had two kids. Beau and Bella. Life was awesome and we're a family. The limited evolution of what others may think about how we feel about our children would not occupy our minds and if we educated some along the way, cool. If not, all is still good in the Sirpilla house.

The following year in our house was out of a fairy tale … at least the fairy tale that we had been dreaming about for 6 years. We hadn't talked about another adoption and another pregnancy was not advised or even foreseeable. Accepting the miracle baby Bella with appreciation beyond measure felt great. We enjoyed having two kids and were so content that we didn't need to discuss more babies …

… until we needed to.

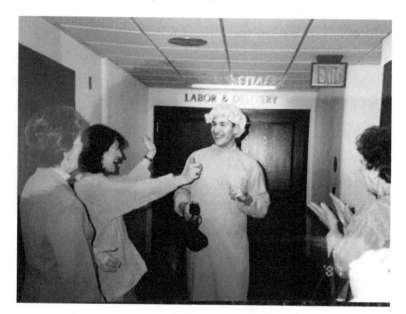

Announcing Bella's birth

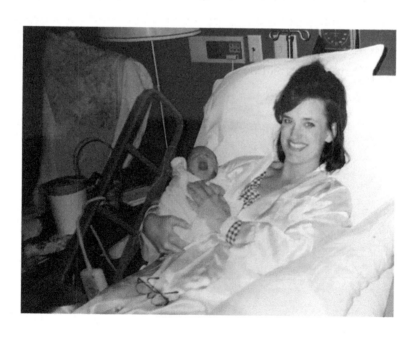

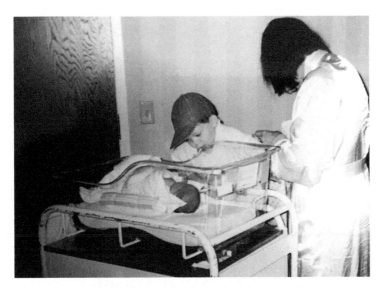

Beau's famous words, "Is her real?"

Bella's first professional photos with her three angels

CHAPTER 16

Lucky Baby #13

"I'm getting a baby brother!"

It was a nice day in late May, and we were in our car with Beau and Bella safely snuggled in their car seats as a friend came up to us in our driveway as we were pulling out. I rolled down the back windows so she could see our sweet kids and Beau made that announcement to her.

Our friend, who had been on this entire journey with us, jumped up and down and said, "Oh my gosh, Susan, you're pregnant?" We looked at one another wide-eyed, smiled and Susan said, "No! I'm not pregnant. I'm not sure why Beau said that." We shrugged it off and went along talking about other things.

Other friends came over who also had a son and daughter and announced that they were pregnant and expecting in February. We were so happy for them and loved them as family. They said that we should consider another, and we laughed it off knowing that we didn't "plan" those things well and were so happy with a one- and three-year-old.

May turned into June and Father's Day rolled around. As I was opening gifts from Susan and the kids, I was literally thinking, "This is crazy! I'm a dad!" At that point, I had been a dad for three years with the kids we were raising and four years including our first three. Yet, it was never lost on me the amazement that "I'm a dad." All I ever wanted to be, and this honor was mine!

As I was unwrapping the last gift, I was barely paying attention to it as I was talking with Susan, Beau, and Bella. The gift box was light, as if nothing was in it, but that fact was lost on me. I was still in shock that I was a dad. As I sifted through the tissue paper, I saw a framed note and a positive pregnancy test.

"You're going to be a dad again!"

Apparently, Beau's comment to our friend about having a baby brother and our other friends telling us about their new pregnancy got Susan thinking. "I haven't had my period in several months, could I be pregnant?" The answer was yes and very pregnant. We needed to get to the doctor!

We accepted being pregnant with Bella as a once in a lifetime miracle. While we heard the clear direction from our doctor that Susan should not be pregnant again for her safety as well as the baby's, at some level we didn't really believe that she would ever get pregnant again. More importantly, we knew that it was God's hand that would guide us, and we were no longer in charge of our child-creating destiny. Our prayer had been for God to send us the children we were meant to raise. We genuinely believed in that prayer, and He would send them to us through whomever He chose. I guess we just didn't think He would pick Susan again.

We returned from our first doctor's appointment with the confirmation that we had a healthy heartbeat and a growing baby. The concern about the tear in Susan's uterus grew larger as it was likely stretched to capacity from the pregnancy with Bella and would be a greater concern in this pregnancy. Knowing that Susan was able to carry Bella to 35 weeks, the doctor felt that complete bed rest wasn't needed until possible concerns arose, but home rest would be our plan. With a one- and three-year-old, Susan would have limitations. Most concerning was the fact that she could not carry them or hold them while standing. Every one and three-year-old wants their mom to hold them ... this was going to be interesting. With the help of our beloved nanny, she would assist Susan at home while I was at work since Susan couldn't be left home alone with the kids. This saddened her with the limitations and restricting Beau and Bella from their normal very active lifestyle. But she knew the risk that she carried and decided, "this too shall pass."

I must admit that the anxiety of a pregnancy is not as intense when you have two small children to soak up your energy and hearts. We had weekly ultrasounds, again restricting them from telling us the sex of the baby, and we were assured the baby was growing well and had a special due date. This baby was due on February 22nd, which was Nicholas, Mary, and Peter's birthday. Of all days! It just seemed as though those three were watching over us and they continued to be with us through our journey for a family. We still looked for those signs, needed them, and felt assurance from them.

We approached this pregnancy with a little less intensity because at some level there was confidence this time. We had an underlying belief that it was going to be okay. This may seem like a callous approach to her 4th pregnancy and our track record to date. This baby was the 13th baby that we were planning for, and we only were raising two in our home, so how could we be calm? Could it really be 13? Let's review:

Nicholas, Mary, and Peter -- #1, #2, #3

The twin pregnancy -- #4, #5

The twin girls in Paraguay -- #6, #7

Jake and Gracie in Paraguay -- #8, #9

Beau -- #10

Beau's birth brother -- #11

Bella -- #12

And now lucky baby #13.

Yet guarded, we were trusting and believed that this baby was coming. At 34 weeks, 6 weeks before her due date, we returned to Aultman Hospital in the caring hands of Dr. Gill for another C-section as Susan was in active labor. Although hesitant, he was obligated to bring up the topic of tying her tubes. With this baby coming even earlier than Bella, his concern was focused on the uterine tear and significant complications ahead. With little thought, we stated that we are thankful that we didn't restrict God's plans for us which brought us this new baby and in good conscience, we couldn't do it again. Our family planning was out of our hands. We made our peace with it, and it didn't require more thinking. We were not blind to the risks ahead but in our seat looking back, we couldn't imagine what we had already been through and if more was ahead, we felt better prepared than ever to face it.

+ + +

In the operating room, the familiar "It's a … "It's a …. BOY!" revealed the birth of our youngest son. Beau was right. He said before we knew Susan was pregnant that his mom was having a baby brother and she did just that. This new little guy quickly had our hearts. He seemed so tiny compared to his older brother and sister, which reminded us of his prematurity and immediate concerns for his health.

He was crying as his head was sticking out of his mother's stomach and the rest of his body was still in utero, so he certainly had healthy lungs. An intensive care team of 12 was in the delivery room prepared to take him to the PICU (pediatric intensive care) but he didn't need it. He was our largest baby to date … Beau at 6 lbs. 3oz, Bella at 6 lbs. 1oz and baby boy at 6 lbs. 7oz. He was 6 weeks early, so he was well on his way to being a big baby if he made it full term.

I was gifted the honor of walking back to the same cast of loving characters to make the announcement. It felt just as great as it did last time, and they were equally happy, shocked, and overwhelmed.

As I said, we didn't know if we were having a boy or a girl and the names that we had landed on for a boy didn't seem to fit this little guy. The birth certificate lady entered the room day after day, but we turned her away without a decision on a name for the certificate. Beau grew impatient and named him "Boy" and for the first three days, that's what we called him. Boy. And it fit him well.

On that Friday night as I was at home with Beau and Bella after getting them to bed, Susan called me with the name she had selected.

Stone.

We hadn't ever discussed the name before, but it sounded right. Stone Christian Sirpilla. Let's ink that on the birth certificate.

Beau and Bella rallied around their baby brother, Stone. We had three children under the age of 4 and life was grand. Better than grand … it was our dream. As time went on and the kids were 5, 3, and 1, people who didn't know us would comment, "Wow, that is perfect family planning. Each kid 2 years apart."

If they only knew …

Johnny's announcement of Stone's birth and embrace with his dad

Johnny and Susan with baby Stone

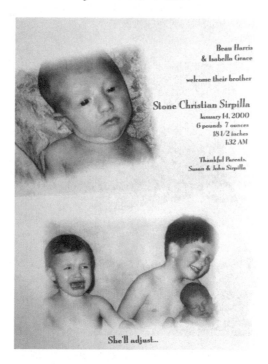

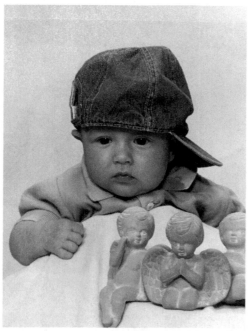

Stone's first professional photos with his three angels

CHAPTER 17

What Have We Done?

Life with kids ages 2, 4, and 6 years old was better than we could have imagined. Stoney was the perfect addition to the family. He was a typical third child, self-sufficient beyond his years, following in the actions of his brother and sister while seemingly carrying his own independence. He became the rule follower, the boy that just didn't get in trouble and when he did, he typically self-disciplined with a trip to the corner. We'd often ask why he was there. He'd reply with an innocent confession of something he "thought" that wasn't nice. We'd ask if he learned his lesson (self-taught) and while holding back grins in our reply, tell him he could come out of the self-imposed "time-out". Raising him really never got harder than that.

Bella had a strength typical of a young girl in between two brothers yet clearly the girl of the bunch. Her brothers were raised to realize that Bella would learn how to be treated by a man based on the way that I treat her and then how her brothers treat her. We are the first men in her life and setting an example for the men that follow was a priority to us. If they needed to yield so she could feel special, they grew to do it naturally and I loved watching young gentlemen in the making.

Few things were more important to me than preparing her to be strong, confident and realize that she was special. She deserved in return the love and kindness that she naturally put into the world. She gracefully accepted and leaned into Beau being protective over her. She in turn, played the same role for Stone and was equally aggressive as her older brother at times.

Beau naturally assumed the role of consummate big brother. He displayed a need for affection with hugs and kisses to his younger brother and sister that was unusual for a tough young boy. He was a big kid with a bigger heart. I never had to ask him to look out for his little sister to ensure boys treated her well. He just did it and as the teen years came, he typically overdid it, but it made me super happy. For Stone, he wanted to encourage him in sports and developed a natural rule in the house that a ball could solve boredom quickly. Stone followed in those steps easily. Beau has led the way in the focusing on the importance of family, our history and what it means to be a Sirpilla.

The dynamic between Beau, Bella and Stone was easy. Sibling tensions were at a minimum and we worked to keep it that way. We were strict with the words they used to engage with each other. A screaming fight was not an option nor seen as "the way that siblings talk to each other." They could disagree, get frustrated, but talk kindly to each other to express their thoughts. We jumped on this bandwagon early, so it really didn't take a lot of effort, reasonably monitoring did the trick. They were happy together.

+ + +

As perfect as life appeared from the outside, Susan and I were wrestling with a problem. Remember when I spoke of the research that we did regarding the Catholic church's teachings on invitro fertilization? We understood that the church had opposition with the medical intervention for creation of a human life, but we relied on our hearts being pure with a love for children and moved forward. What we didn't appreciate was a larger view of the complications that could arise from interfering in the creation of human embryos. When we made our decision to take the most extreme medical intervention steps possible, we never would have thought that we would have excess embryos without the ability to use them. We were different than most IVF couples. We produced an extreme number of fertilized embryos ... 22 ... from one cycle and Susan later developed severe medical complications that would put her life in danger ... again ... if she carried another baby. Clearly, not the norm.

We were open to having more children. I actually wanted three more and at the very least, one more. Susan was content with Beau, Bella, and Stone but open to what God had planned for us. The message from our doctor that came at

Stone's delivery regarding another pregnancy for Susan was deliberate and clear. She could not withstand another pregnancy and the risks had exponentially increased after two extremely high-risk pregnancies resulting in premature, yet healthy babies. We had two unplanned pregnancies in 19 months. Were we now a couple that needed to try to avoid pregnancies? It almost sounded ridiculous because we had spent so many years being the infertility couple and we were now a fertile couple without the ability to safely have another baby. With our faith leading us away from contraception for 10 years of our marriage, we weren't willing to go against that practice, so we would need to "be careful."

The bigger issue rested in the laboratory freezers at the Cleveland hospital with 12 Sirpilla baby embryos. If they can't go safely in Susan and in a time where surrogacy was just developing but not common practice, we saw four options:

One: Keep them in the freezer for eternity. This could mean that 100 years from now, someone could have access to our embryos and who knows what would happen to them.

Two: Give them to another couple. While a loving gesture certainly, we couldn't get there.

Three: Destroy them. Absolutely, not an option that would merit any discussion.

Four: Put them in Susan against the strong medical advice that would put Susan's life at risk and the baby's as well.

What have we done?

Our mothers were adamant in their stance that Susan not become pregnant again. My mother more aggressively than Susan's, which was a natural reflection of my mother's intensity and her mother's calmer demeanor. On more than one occasion since Stone's birth we were asked if we were being careful to avoid another pregnancy. Their pleas were from their heart with the focus on their grandchildren.

"Beau, Bella, and Stone need their mother. You can't risk them growing up without Susan. Johnny, don't let this happen!"

I was never offended by their expression of concern. Some might see it as mother's meddling in our affairs but let's be fair here. They were on this ENTIRE journey with us. They endured the stress for the past six years. They lived in worry. They suffered loss. This just wasn't about us and that was clear to me. Our village earned the right to voice their opinions and let us know how they felt, and it would be wrong to deny them what they felt compelled to share. We relied on them constantly for years. Could we really shut them out because they were making statements of the obvious? While they shared our faith, they didn't share our tolerance for what we had risked getting a house filled with three little characters that stole our hearts.

Through frequent prayer, meetings with our priest, and many sessions with Dr. Barb Fordyce, we processed our options. Barb understood our hearts, our life-threatening dilemma, and the core of our souls to do the right thing despite heavy circumstances. Her guidance was needed yet again 10 years later, and she never let us down. In time, we knew what we had to do. The only place that the embryos could go was where they were meant to be … in their mother's womb.

Now, the tough part … getting our doctor to agree.

It was time to return to the secrecy in our family planning as we did in the early years. This was a journey we needed to take alone and not put those we loved through more of our challenges. We met with our trusted friend, Dr. Prab Gill, and turned to him for his constant source of wisdom.

Dr. Gill, a man of high moral fiber, listened intently, heard every angle that we could imagine and realized we were troubled to our core. He educated us again on the risks of a fifth pregnancy and then came up with a solution that we all could live with. Knowing our concern for the countless drugs that Susan endured to get pregnant and stay pregnant, he thought of a more natural path in this unnatural path of creation. We would thaw the embryos two at a time and place them in Susan on the typical day of conception, day 14 of her cycle. We would not inject her body with hormones to assist with the perfect circumstances for her uterine lining to be prepared for implantation, rather we would allow nature to take its course. The embryos would return to where they would be in a natural conception setting and God would take it from there. If Susan became pregnant, she would later be placed on bed rest, and we would take it one day at a time. If she did not, we would return the following cycle until each embryo that had successfully thawed was returned to their natural habitat.

Over the many months ahead, we took these steps knowing that we were doing the right thing and trusting that God would continue to be with us. We went through hopeful weeks dreaming of a new child, yet relief when we knew Susan was safe and not pregnant, and then geared up for another cycle. We never conceived through those attempts, but our hearts were at ease. We honored the souls that we created while understanding the greater perspective the Catholic faith had with a full circle view of the complications that can arise by tampering with our fertility.

We have no judgment for anyone who fully pursues the medical options available to them in their struggle for a family. Different faiths have different views on this topic, and we respect that. Our path clearly does not serve as the easy path "how to" guide to build a family. The struggle is personal and unique to each couple, their faith, and their values. For us, we accepted that although well intentioned, we created a situation that we could not ignore. Lurking in our happy home of five was the sense that we were not complete with 12 Sirpilla embryos awaiting their fate. As tough as it was, we faced it and made the best decision for us with God's grace.

Now a family of five

REFLECTION

Balloons, Love Letters and Gratitude

Would we have done things differently?

Probably.
Maybe.
I don't know.

All I know is that our prayers were answered. We prayed for God to send us the children He intended for us to raise. And we raised them with a lot of love and laughter ... it felt amazing. In that, we found an understanding for our path, comfort in our pain, and abundance of gratitude for the life we've had as a family.

Beau, Bella, and Stone are now three young adults and remain the center of our lives. They all chose the same college, High Point University, in North Carolina, the birthplace for the title of this book. Bella was a senior, Stone, a sophomore, and in attendance on that fateful day when I was asked what I wish I knew when I sat in their seats as a college student.

Beau graduated the year before and introduced our family to the university that became our home away from home for eight consecutive years. It was there where we met and befriended, Dr. Nido Qubein, author of the Foreword to this book and President of High Point University. He created the environment to further enrich our children with a quality education and better yet, what the university is known for … teaching life skills.

Now, they all live in downtown Chicago pursuing their careers. While each having their independence, there is a sense of home they feel in being together and that is just fine with us. They love and honor their older brothers and sister, Nicholas, Mary, and Peter. We've celebrated their birthday for the past 27 years and continue to keep their memory alive. The "original three" were born boy, girl, and boy and then we received the next boy, girl, and boy to raise. Beau and Nicholas shared the role of big brother and protectors, Mary and Bella's features and habits that take my breath away, and Stone and Peter … St. Peter, the rock of the church, and our Stone, the stable rock in our family.

On Beau's third birthday, he begged me to allow Nicholas, Mary, and Peter to come down from heaven to attend his birthday party. The sweetness in his request was more than I could handle, and it led to something beautiful. While disappointed that they couldn't attend, he wanted to send them the balloons from his party so they could be part of the celebration. And that became a tradition for every one of our kid's birthday parties. On the triplet's birthday we continue to send up two blue and one pink balloon to the heavens. We did it as a family when we all lived together and since the kids left for college and beyond, we unite through FaceTime so the five of us can continue the tradition. We share our appreciation for the guardian angels that they have always been and cannot picture our lives without them beside us. I did get the six kids that I always wanted and have come to appreciate the unique way in which I have them.

As a gesture of appreciation for God allowing me to be the father to three amazing young people, I started writing a love letter to each of them when they were born and surprised them with it on each of their 18th birthdays. Each of their first 18 years of memories, emotions, and feelings I had are documented in hardback books. I wanted them to know their dad's heart --- how deeply I loved them and how they fulfilled my greatest purpose in life. Over two hundred pages each, single spaced and typed, the love letters along with photos for each time period serve as reminder to Beau, Bella, and Stone what they mean to me.

While writing this book in my early to mid 50's, I look back at the young couple in the chapters and have an unusual perspective. As I proofread chapters that I wrote, I found myself being shocked by the story with empathy for the younger version of ourselves. At times, it felt that it all happened to a couple that I'm close to and my heart aches for them. And then a harsh reality hits that it *is* our story and that *was* our path. Maybe that is a way that our brain protects us subconsciously, but we're okay looking back at them while still being them.

More than anything, I was determined to not fall victim to tragedy and hard times. That path was too dark for me, and I felt low and discouraged in those thoughts. Barb's teachings to reframe our thoughts forever changed me. I could have been the dad and husband who is forever angry for our loss. How tough it would be to live the next 50 years seeing life through those lenses.

Or, I could be the dad and husband who was blessed enough to experience a life changing event that allowed my heart to shape, expand and prepare for the deep feelings that being a committed dad and husband could offer. I'm so blessed for the path it took for us to become a family. It changed me in every possible way for the better. My outlook on life, my marriage, and my business has all benefited from reframing my many thoughts to work for me as opposed to against me. It is a daily process to keep that frame of mind but one that never lets me down.

Nicholas, Mary, and Peter gave me the gift of loving their mother more deeply by watching her endure so much. What an amazing gift to receive in my twenties and benefit from it growing for over 30 years of marriage. Susan was a warrior, relentless in what she would endure (including tolerating my intensity), and a faithful servant to God. Words don't exist for me to thank her for the way that she mothered our children. Their strength and sensibility come from her, and I have leaned on her more than I could ever imagined. From being the college senior meeting her when I thought I had life all figured out and believed how much I could "catch her up" with my intensity for life and getting things done, to the man that realizes how often I would be down if she didn't pick me up. I'm a lucky guy.

I'm certain that Nicholas, Mary, and Peter and our journey prepared me for the life in business that I had. It became natural to connect to the people that I served and led because I knew that they too had their stories that shaped them. I hope in some way that I was able to assist in reframing their personal and professional thoughts to their greatest benefit. I felt an honor and responsibility to thousands of committed, hardworking associates to ensure their careers were successful. I felt that was my primary job as their leader; make them successful.

Those lessons could be an entirely new book and that might just happen.

Even after our family was formed, life continued to be hard. While filled with an abundance of love and blessings, we've faced severe illnesses for all three kids that they carry with them to this day. They deal with their challenges with resilience, have never lived in the "why me?" moment, and fight with courage and strength. They give me energy for the battles ahead.

They are the next generation proving that *Life is Hard* ...

... But now I really do know, *They Will Be Ok.*

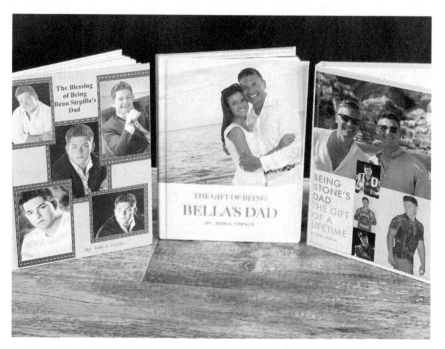

18 years of individual love letters to Beau, Bella, and Stone are bound in their own book for their 18th birthdays. The books followed them to college, and now as adults in Chicago. I love the unexpected text messages I receive as they still go back and randomly read the letters and offer their own reflections many years later.

Family FaceTime for balloon sendoff

AFTERWORD

by Dr. Barb Fordyce, Ph.D.

When I think of Johnny and Susan, I think of La dolce vita (the sweet life). Throughout their journey in life together, they have invested in relationships with family, close friends, and their community. That along with their strong faith, grateful attitudes, and appreciation for the blessings in life as well as acceptance that life is often challenging, has allowed them to become resilient and to find a sense of purpose and meaning. In their attempts to create the family they both wished for beyond anything else, they "bounced back" more often than most people can imagine. In the pursuit of their dreams, they were often met with hope initially. Too often, they met obstacles that dashed those dreams, or how they would have envisioned them. Their story is one of great joy, sorrow, perseverance, growth, and amazing faith.

I remember the day that I first met Johnny nearly 30 years ago. We spoke after my presentation to Leadership Stark County. He was very interested in the cognitive behavioral theory and strategies that I presented. It seemed to resonate for him, and we chatted at length about its application in living a balanced life. Of particular interest to him was the concept of cognitive reframing, an extremely useful tool that he and Susan relied upon and found to be very valuable as they dealt with grief and loss numerous times.

I have had the honor to share sacred parts of their lives as a professional and as a friend. Over the course of years of knowing each other and navigating the many twists and turns that life has brought in all of our lives, we have grown up in the same community as volunteers and friends. About ten years ago, Johnny and I decided to launch a speaking platform that blends psychological strategies and life stories with many audiences in order to help others lead their lives as individuals as well as leaders. Our first event was "Lead Your Life", which was a community talk open to the public. The response was overwhelming. That led to numerous other speaking events and the development of workshops and seminars for organizations and businesses that focus on psychology, workplace wellness, and leadership training. I have often said that I present psychological content and Johnny brings it alive with his stories about life and leadership.

As individuals and as a couple, Susan and Johnny have been perfect role models for demonstrating the many strategies that comprise resilience. With the right tools and supports in place, they not only made it through the many challenges of their journey, but they also emerged more confident and courageous. I am deeply honored to write this afterword for their beautifully written and heartfelt life story. And who knows...at some point they may wish to share more chapters in the story of their lives together.

Be well on your journey,
Barbara Fordyce, Ph.D.
Psychologist

Psychological Principles & Strategies
Used by Johnny & Susan
By: Barbara Fordyce, Ph.D.
Psychologist

I am including some of the strategies for resilience that Johnny and Susan relied upon and modeled for their children and many others along their journey through life. These are also some of the areas that Johnny and I highlight in our presentations.

Psychologists define resilience as the process of adapting well in the face of adversity, trauma, tragedy, threats, or significant sources of stress—such as family and relationship problems, serious health problems, or workplace and financial stressors. As much as resilience involves "bouncing back" from these difficult experiences, it can also involve profound personal growth.

While these adverse events are certainly painful and difficult, they don't have to determine the outcome of our lives. There are many aspects of our lives that we can control or modify that promote growth and improved quality of life. While certain factors might make some individuals more resilient than others, resilience isn't necessarily a personality trait that only some people possess. On the contrary, resilience involves behaviors, thoughts, and actions that anyone can learn and develop. Increasing resilience takes time and intentionality. Focusing on four core components—wellness, social support, healthy thinking, and finding positive meaning—can empower us to withstand and learn from difficult and traumatic experiences.

Wellness

Take care of your body. Self-care may be a popular buzzword, but it's also a legitimate practice for mental health and building resilience. That's because stress is just as much physical as it is emotional. Promoting positive lifestyle factors like proper nutrition, ample sleep, hydration, and regular exercise can strengthen your body to adapt to stress and reduce the toll of emotions like anxiety or depression.

Practice mindfulness. Mindful journaling, yoga, and other spiritual practices like prayer or meditation can also help people build connections and restore hope, which can assist them in dealing with situations that require resilience. Whether you journal, meditate, or pray, focus on positive aspects of your life and recall the things you're grateful for, even during personal trials.

Research suggests that a simple gratitude practice, such as writing down a few things you're grateful for every day, can change the "wiring" in your brain and may increase optimism, overall well-being, and willpower. Focus on giving your body resources to manage stress.

Social Support

Build your connections and prioritize relationships. Connecting with empathetic and understanding people can remind you that you're not alone in the midst of difficulties. Focus on finding trustworthy and compassionate individuals who honor your feelings, which will support the skill of resilience.

The correlation between flourishing and enjoying good social relationships is so strong and reliable that scientists have called it a necessary condition for flourishing. Social support is a necessary factor in developing resilience and coping skills.

Join a group. Along with one-on-one relationships, some people find that being active in civic groups, faith-based communities, or other local organizations provides social support and can help you reclaim hope. Research groups in your area that could offer you support and a sense of purpose or joy when you need it.

Whether you volunteer within your community or simply support a friend in their time of need, you can garner a sense of purpose, foster self-worth, connect with other people, and tangibly help others, all of which can empower you to grow in resilience.

Move toward your goals. Develop some realistic goals and do something regularly—even if it seems like a small accomplishment—that enables you to move forward. Instead of focusing on tasks that seem unattainable ask yourself, "What's one thing I know I can accomplish today that helps me move in the direction I want to go?"

Healthy Thinking

Keep things in perspective. How you think can play a significant part in how you feel—and how resilient you are when faced with obstacles. Try to identify areas of irrational thinking, such as a tendency to catastrophize difficulties, and adopt a more balanced and realistic thinking pattern. If you are feeling overwhelmed by a challenge, remind yourself that what happened to you isn't an indicator of how your future will go and that you're not helpless or hopeless. You may not be able to change a highly stressful event, but you can change how you interpret and respond to it. Cognitive reframing is a psychological technique that consists of identifying and then changing the way situations, experiences, events, ideas, and/or emotions are viewed. Cognitive reframing is the process by which such situations or thoughts are challenged and then changed.

Cognitive restructuring is a technique that has been successfully used to help people change the way they think.

When used for stress management, the goal is to replace stress-producing thoughts (cognitive distortions) with more balanced thoughts that do not produce stress.

Challenge your thinking by asking yourself the following questions:

Is this thought realistic?

Am I basing my thoughts on facts or on feelings?

What is the evidence for this thought?

Could I be misinterpreting the evidence?

Am I viewing the situation as black and white when it's really more complicated?

Am I having this thought out of habit or do facts support it?

Finding Positive Meaning

Find positive meaning more frequently in your day-to-day life circumstances. Most of the circumstances in life that we face are not totally negative. Try to find some part of the situation that is good, even if it's simply to realize that "this too shall pass" When we reframe unpleasant circumstances in a positive way, we boost the odds that positive emotions, like hope will flow forth.

Connect with nature. Studies show that people can put themselves on healing trajectories by spending time outdoors connecting to nature.

Accept change. Accept that change is a part of life. Certain goals or ideals may no longer be attainable as a result of adverse situations in your life. Accepting circumstances that cannot be changed can help you focus on circumstances that you can alter.

Maintain a hopeful outlook. An optimistic outlook empowers you to expect that good things will happen to you. Try visualizing what you want rather than worrying about what you fear. Along the way, note any subtle ways in which you start to feel better as you deal with difficult situations.

Learn from your past. By looking back at who or what was helpful in previous times of distress, you may discover how you can respond effectively to new difficult situations. Remind yourself of where you've been able to find strength and ask yourself what you've learned from those experiences.

Seeking help when you need it is crucial in building your resilience. For many people, using the kinds of strategies listed above may be enough for building their resilience. But at times, when it's difficult to make progress on the road to resilience, a licensed mental health professional can assist in developing appropriate strategies for moving forward. It is important to get professional help if you feel like you are unable to function as well as you would like or perform basic activities of daily living as a result of a traumatic or other stressful life experience.

The important thing is to remember you're not alone on the journey. While you may not be able to control all of your circumstances, you can grow by focusing on the aspects of life's challenges that you can manage with the support of loved ones and trusted professionals.

ACKNOWLEDGEMENTS

I never imagined myself as an author but as our lives unfolded and we shared our story, we were greeted with a universal ... "you have to write a book". The seed was planted. As I continued to refer to those dark days as a point of reference for managing my current thoughts, I see the growth and perspective that was provided to us through the heartache and eventually, joy. When I retired from my thirty-year career in the RV industry and decided to follow my passions in the "second half" of my career, I knew the book would find its way to the fountain of passions that were now accessible due to the luxury of time.

However, without my children's insistence that I spend more time on the book, I don't think this project would have been completed. Their encouragement and quite honestly, their expectation that I follow through with the challenge of putting to paper what we had experienced became an inspiration to me. I've challenged them repeatedly in their lives and now the tables turned, and I was being challenged by them. I could not let them down. Beau, Bella, and Stone, thank you for your belief in the importance of honoring what your mom and I endured so we could be a family. What we share today is the reward for the journey and I'd do it all again. Most importantly, thank you for loving Nicholas, Mary and Peter and the roles that you have all played in keeping them a part of our family. You honor my commitment to having their brief lives be ones of significance and never forgotten.

To my wife, Susan. I'd say "no words" … but this is a book, so I need to find those words. ☺ Your determination became mine. My intensity became yours. And together we built a family. Your quiet strength and ability to find calm in the storms sustained me. The way I love you today is so much more intense than it was 30 years ago which is a tribute to your selfless heart and what you have done for our family. We certainly have proven that life is hard but with you by my side, I'm better than ok … I'm complete.

To my family and village. I was blessed to be born into a family of deep commitment to each other. My mom and dad, my sisters, Renae and Laura and their amazing families, you all carried us in the times that we needed you most. Every gesture of love, concern and support has never been forgotten. You led the way with your own families and gave us nieces, nephews and now their spouses that feel like our own. Those young people filled our lives and gave us hope. The way you adore Susan, Beau, Bella, and Stone is the definition of family. I won the lottery being born as a Sirpilla and that has never been lost on me.

To our chosen family and village that was formed nearly 30 years ago through our St. Michael's faith group bible study. You are our faith family. The family we built together. I know that our friendship was difficult during those years, and we laughed at times that it was even hard to be friends with us. Too many tough life experiences to share in a span of 6+ years but you never left our side. Rallying at the hospital, endless meals of comfort food, and being ready for what awaited us at the next turn. You never left our side and along the way created the greatest treasures in our kid's lives … their closest friends that are your children. To have the second generation of faith family growing and creating the third generation is beyond a gift. I love watching them continue to grow and love each other as family. We built something special.

To our family and friends, old and new, who continue to honor those days, showing interest and concern as we have told our story. Your patience as the story can consume an evening keeps us connected to that young couple who had big dreams for family and friends like you.

To the countless medical professionals who held our hands, guided us and were always in our corner. You offered hope when we felt hopeless which gave us strength that we desperately needed.

To Bill Butterworth, my new friend in this journey to pen our trials. I didn't want a ghost writer because I wanted to write this book with words that were mine and authentic. Your thoughtful review of my writing, edits, and guidance to complete this book created a special bond between us. You're a talented storyteller and I've learned so much from you.

To Elite Publishing. Melanie, Jenn and the team became friends in the journey, and you brought this book to life and publication. I enjoyed our collaboration and Zoom calls to ensure each detail was addressed. We had some fun and made good decisions along the way.

Then vs. now

ABOUT THE AUTHOR

Johnny Sirpilla is an entrepreneur, author, and speaker. He speaks professionally to businesses, communities, and universities on the importance of managing thoughts, internal honest reflection to develop meaningful professional and personal relationships and re-framing each challenge in your life as an opportunity for self-development and growth. Addressing college students, young professionals, and emerging leaders to discover the power they must develop for their personal brand is one of his passions. He has been an active community leader serving as Chairman of the Board for the United Way of Greater Stark County, Chairman of the Board for Stark County Catholic Schools, Executive Committee Member & Board Member of the Aultman Health Foundation, Executive Committee Member and Board Member of the Pro Football Hall of Fame and board member of The Pregnancy Support Center. He received the Jackson Chamber of Commerce Outstanding Citizen of the Year.

Johnny is the owner of Encourage, LLC. and the retired President and Chief Business Development Officer of Camping World and Good Sam. He graduated Miami University in 1988 with a bachelor's degree in accounting, a minor in Finance and a special interest in psychology and received his master's in Organizational Behavioral Management in 2000 from University of Phoenix. In 2022, he received certification from the University of Pennsylvania Wharton School in Executive Presence and Influence & Persuasive Leadership Development.

Johnny's experience in business leadership began in 1992 when he became President of Sirpilla R.V. Center, Inc. and was recognized out of 3,000 dealers as the National RV Dealer of the Year for best overall run dealership in the country in 1995. In 2003, he was one of the initial acquisitions by Camping World and served in key executive leadership roles of the $4 billion revenue business for 14 years prior to his retirement. He currently runs his family office, Encourage LLC, which has holdings in several industries including e-commerce consolidations, fashion and interior design, spirit brands, senior housing, med-tech device, and population health management. Johnny is co-founder/board member for Society Brands, board member of TecTraum, board member of publicly traded Lippert Components (LCII) and an active leadership consultant.

Johnny has been married to his college sweetheart, Susan, for over 30 years and has three grown children, Beau, Bella, and Stone. They reside in Canton, Ohio and Naples, Florida with their two dogs, Ted and Luna-Mae.

For more information visit Encourage33.com

Made in the USA
Columbia, SC
30 June 2022